LETTERS TO A FRIEND

Simple Lessons in Christian Living

GREGORY E. LANG

For Harper, Sutton, and Patrick

*"My home is in Heaven.
I'm just traveling through this world."*

BILLY GRAHAM

Table of Contents

Dear Beloved Friend,

I WRITE THESE little letters to give you advice that will keep you in the right relationship with God. A right relationship with God is more important than anything else you might enjoy in this world, but without proper attention, it can be elusive for many of your days. I want to help spare you any separation from God. My friend, there is an ongoing war between good and evil that will endure for a time, and your very soul is the object of this conflict. This war is not always obvious; it is often played out in subtle maneuvers on the battlefields of your heart and mind. The enemy utilizes so many distractions and falsehoods in this war that it would be easy for you to become preoccupied with pondering immediate and empirical things rather than things unseen and of a time beyond the here and now. I want your life to be of the utmost purpose, meaning, and peace that will last forever, so I want to teach you these few important lessons while I can about how to guard yourself against defeat by the attacks of this enemy.

My letters are more about what you should do and how to be in this world during this war than they are explanations for the inevitable *Why* questions that will arise during your daily struggles. It is perfectly fine to ask why questions; I have so many times myself, and truthfully, I often still do. But I think it better for you to begin acting like a Christian as soon as you can rather than wait until you are intellectually satisfied with theological answers to your questions. I think this because I believe God smiles on your good conduct even if you may not know the doctrine supporting your actions. As God smiles on you, you will enjoy his blessings, and those blessings will urge you to continue your good deeds, which, in turn, helps to open your heart and mind to explanations that might otherwise escape your understanding. This is your strategy for prevailing triumphant in this war, to discern and obey the will of God.

You may think my letters are repetitious, but the truth deserves repeating, and often. Practice makes perfect. All these lessons may not be believable and relatable to you just yet. Still, I promise, if you heed my advice and return to these letters often, your heart and mind will slowly be opened to an incomprehensible wonder you cannot ignore. This is my hope for you, that you will know the Lord as I do, for that would mean we will one day be together in fellowship in Heaven into eternity. Oh, what a victorious blessing that will be! I thank God for you and pray that he and my letters will comfort you throughout your life. May it be so!

In the beginning, God created the heavens and the earth.

GENESIS 1:1

*The heavens declare the glory of God;
and the firmament shows His handiwork.*

PSALM 19:1

Awe of God

FRIEND, LET US begin at the beginning. What better place in the whole collection of God-breathed words to encounter our first conflict between God and the world than Genesis 1:1. I tell you the truth: these ten words are pivotal to your journey through the remainder of your coming to know God. The foundation of Christianity is laid in our relation to God as our Creator. If you do not believe Genesis 1:1 without any qualification or rationalization, if you cannot take the verse on its face and believe that God is the origin, the author, of all things, that he needed no help to turn nothing into something, and not just any something but something as grand and splendorous as the star-filled galaxy and the vestibular system within your inner ears that keeps you upright in that galaxy as the world spins on its axis at more than 1000 miles per hour, you will gain little if anything from my letters.

God—the name of the Supreme Being. One of the main themes of Genesis is to establish the sovereignty of God. The sovereignty, the full right and power to govern oneself without any interference from outside sources, of God. There is absolutely nothing that happens in the universe that is outside of God's influence and authority. As King of kings and Lord of lords, God has no limitations. The sovereignty of God is not merely that God has the power and right to govern all things but that He does govern all things, always and without exception. God is not simply sovereign in principle but sovereign in practice.

Genesis 1:1 affirms God alone is eternal and that all else owes its origin and existence to him. No doubt, the very first verse of the Bible is a major stumbling block for those who place their faith in science. Your first surrender during this journey is to accept what you may not understand as truth and to believe in God and what he says. If you fail to do that, you hold science in higher esteem than God. You must not attempt to reduce the nonreducible; you cannot comprehend the ways of God. You must worship him by faith rather than evidence. As a wise man once said, "If you understand, it is not God." (St. Augustine)

The real danger of dismissing the miracle of creation is that such thoughts introduce doubt about the truth of the whole Bible. Doubt is insidious and pervasive, a great arrow in the enemy's sheath. Doubt about the truth of Genesis 1:1 will lead you to doubt that Adam was formed from dirt and Eve from his rib. When you dismiss these and all other miracles, you put aside the very evidence given to you that should leave you with your mouth dropped in awe of God.

But you are tempted to understand the miracles of the Bible with the aid of science, aren't you? Be warned: do not burden your mind with efforts to fuse science and the word of God; such is to attempt a peace accord between God's truth and man's knowledge. Such is to believe the knowledge of man is equal to the wisdom of God. It is not necessary here to discredit science but to put it in its proper place, and that place is not just after God but also beneath God.

An abundance of scientific evidence suggests the universe had a beginning. If there was a beginning, there was a cause for that beginning. Since the beginning, we have had a very complex universe, an intricate system of cause-and-effect forces that work together for the mutual benefit of the whole. The Earth is not breaking down before our eyes and devolving into random chaos, but it is stable, sustained, and predictable; the Earth and its living creatures are an amalgam of particularities that work together according to a design—a masterful design—not by chance.

There was a cause that brought about a beginning that resulted in something that is the product of a masterful design. What was that cause? We cannot say it was something else without falling into the trap of explaining one beginning with an endless regression of causes that begot other beginnings, predating the beginning that resulted in us. According to God, he created the heavens and the earth; they were not formed from any pre-existing materials but made from nothing. Again, be in awe!

Only something that had no beginning but rather always was and is and will be could be the agent that caused the beginning, and that would be God. God is the uncaused cause of all finite things. When Moses asked God for his name, his response was " "I Am Who I Am". It is clear God determines God; no one or anything else does. God is omnipotent (can do anything), omnipresent (is everywhere), and omniscient (knows everything), and on that divine authority, in the beginning, he created the heavens and the earth.

In the beginning of time, this world was created by a Being of infinite wisdom and power, who was himself before all time and all worlds. This first verse declares the great and important truth that all things had a beginning, that nothing throughout the vast extent of nature existed from eternity, originated by chance, or from the skill of any inferior agent, but that God's creative power produced the whole universe. God made heaven and earth out of nothing. The world was not eternal but had a beginning, and its creation was caused only by the power and wisdom of God, the first cause and sole author of all things.

Lay everything else aside, take a step in faith, and embrace Genesis 1:1, the first documented miracle, given to you so that you may know your Father's awe-inspiring power and unfathomable brilliance. It is your first step in surrendering to God.

Everyone who is called by my name,
whom I created for my glory,
whom I formed and made.

Isaiah 43:5-7

Your Purpose

FRIEND, THIS LETTER brings you a lesson of immeasurable importance; consider this carefully. As I have already told you, the foundation of Christianity is built upon our proper relation to God as our Creator. You must understand that you are not your own; you belong to God. You are a splendid jar of clay made with his very hands. He designed and formed you. And just as you are not your own, your purpose in this world is not your own; instead, it belongs to God. God's purpose for you is your only ordained purpose. Your ordained purpose is the very reason you were created, and you were created to glorify God. You have but one objective in life: to please the Lord through praise and worship of him. God owes you nothing, but you owe him everything!

Therefore, do not seek anything other than the glory of God and his approval of you. Spend your time and energy in constant devotion to him, giving your whole life to his praise and glory, pressing through every difficulty in your path in faithful pursuit of fulfilling your purpose. Then, not only will you please God, but he will show you his pleasure, fill you with hope, and prosper you with Heavenly blessings. Friend, blessings on Earth are one thing, but those that await you in Heaven far exceed the riches of this world! Please, do not lust and labor for worldly treasures for your gratification today, for not one of them will sustain you. Only your Creator sustains you; he is worthy of your every effort, ceaseless praise, and undivided devotion.

This is a difficult teaching, but learn it you must. To glorify God, much is required of you. For example, you must always be willing to go to uncomfortable places or endure uncomfortable experiences if doing so brings credit and praise for the Lord. Never tolerate any avoidance of your purpose in yourself. Never self-indulge in any practice or opinion that is not agreeable to a holy God. Always be aware of every thought on your mind and the words coming from your mouth, and let both be an example to others of what a God-honoring life looks like. Take no credit for being a good person; do nothing for your praise and glory, for you cannot save yourself. Jesus, the manifestation of God in the flesh, has done that work for you. So instead, praise God that he holds you upright in his mighty and merciful hand.

I know it is tempting to think you know what is best for you and to imagine what will be your lasting legacy. But your legacy will not last, for all worldly things pass away and are forgotten over time. Only Heavenly things will endure. It is far better that your legacy be that you had the saving knowledge of Christ, as shown by your loyal, heartfelt obedience to his commands. Strive to know his commands and abide in them. They are quite simple: "Love the Lord your God with all your heart and with all your soul and with all your strength and with all your mind, and love your neighbor as yourself." Do that, and you will live *forever*.

Remember always that you are an image-bearer of the Almighty God. You were created to bring glory to him, to honor him, to praise his name, to thank him for his abundance in your life, and to praise him for his endless grace, the riches of his love, his splendor, and majesty as a God who is righteous and just. This is the very purpose of man – to glorify God in every way, all of the time. Go to him daily in reverence and awe and willfully submit to your purpose!

Again, Child of God, give glory to God in Christ and represent him well. Remember, your Father in Heaven wants to bless you, prosper you, and help you find joy in all his creation because he loves you. Where else might you find a love such as this! It is fitting, then, I think, to give yourself entirely to him and his plans for you in a spirit of thanksgiving and posture of obedience. If you agree, and I pray you do, labor for the Lord, making him known through your righteous words and deeds, and praise him in your thoughts and words. I encourage you as a friend and one who loves you to accept, embrace, and fulfill your purpose. Thanks be to God for all that you will accomplish in his name. Amen.

*For we ourselves have heard Him
and we know that this is indeed the Christ,
the Savior of the world.*

JOHN 4:42B

Jesus

MY FRIEND, THE subject of this letter, Jesus, is of immeasurable importance. Please take a deep breath, clear your mind of all distractions, and pay close attention to what I am about to teach you, for it is a challenging thing to comprehend. In fact, it is quite difficult to condense all that can be understood about Jesus into a single brief letter, so I urge you to consider this only a primer. If my teaching appeals to you at all, commit yourself to learning more through your study and curiosity. You will be richly rewarded for the time you spend discovering more about Jesus.

Now, on to the reason I am writing to you. You are a broken person living in a broken world and, as such, are constantly bombarded by the temptation of sin. In the exercise of your free will, you inevitably do the very things you ought not to do. Your sin renders you unclean and unholy in the sight of God, thus you

16

are rightly separated from him. How is it, then, that a broken and unholy person can glorify a God who demands perfection in his creature? You may aspire to holiness, but sadly, you will never achieve it because you, as am I, are cursed with an inherited sin nature passed down to us through our disobedient forefathers, beginning with Adam. As much effort as you may invest in being good, you can never be good enough, for the weakness of the flesh will always fail you. Therefore, what to do? Friend, you need an advocate to represent you before God, and in fact, you have the perfect one in Jesus Christ.

Jesus Christ, the Son of God, our advocate, is your Savior. He is your Savior because only he, who is God himself on Earth in the form of man, is able to protect you from the just punishment you, a sinner, are due. Although born into a broken world, Jesus was not conceived by man. Thus, he had no sin nature, and without a sin nature he was able to obey God completely and with absolute perfection. Thus blameless because he violated not one of God's commandments (was without sin), he stands before God on the merit of his righteousness. And in his unlimited and uncompromising love for you, knowing your weaknesses and inabilities, he gave himself as a willing sacrifice for the benefit of you, indeed for all men, to pay the penalty of sin so that you might live in Heaven in the presence of God where you will glorify him, just as intended. Wonderful! Yes, but how is this amazing thing accomplished?

If the wages of sin are death, and you and I, as sinners, are surely destined to die, what is the reward for living a life absent of sin? Life! Jesus, the lamb without blemish who was slain, defeated death, and is now in the company of God where he, stirred by his love for you, through grace (unmerited favor), extends his boundless righteous credit to cover your debt when you profess your belief that the sufficiency of Jesus Christ's sacrifice is far more than enough to overshadow, indeed erase, your guilt as a sinner. Christ satisfied the wrath of God once and for all time. God is so pleased in the faith and work of Christ that his good pleasure overflows and reaches all men who cling to Christ as their hope for eternal survival. Yes, Christ died in this world so that dead men might live with him in the next. This is an invaluable offer, and I beg you to accept it.

Friend, it took me a long time to understand this, and it might for you, too. I pray that you spend time reading the Bible, praying, and fellowshipping with other believers so that what I have written to you may become more believable and irresistible. I pray this because it is my heart's desire that we will enjoy God in Heaven together for eternity. Amen.

For by grace you have been saved through faith,
and that not of yourselves; it is the gift of God,
not of works, lest anyone should boast.

EPHESIANS 2:8-9

Grace

FRIEND, I'M SURE you agree with me that most human interactions are transactional in nature. We exchange value for value and favor for favor. I do something for you, and you do something for me in return. Often, whether openly acknowledged or not, this creates a cycle of indebtedness to one another. I am moved to do something for you because you recently did something for me. I may become unwilling to do more for you because you have not recently returned my favors, so I decide to withhold future favors from you until the reciprocal exchange resumes. In such a dynamic, it is difficult to prove that my motive for engaging with you at all is my love for you rather than my hope for some selfish gain.

I'm writing to tell you, and I want you to believe it, that unlike you, me, and others who look at our fellow man from a perspective of earning and deserving, Jesus always considers us with unconditional love. How wonderful that he does not withhold himself from us until we are obedient and worthy. This is most true when you sincerely ask yourself what can you give him that is fair repayment for what he has done for you? The honest answer is a big nothing. You, as am I, are a sinner who always falls short of the glory of God. Try as you might to live a life without sin, you will always be broken and unworthy. And just as you did not create yourself, neither can you fix yourself. That is why grace is such a wonderful thing. Grace, unmerited favor, is the expression of Christ's unconditional love for you. It is when, even if you are doing the very things you should not do or refuse to do the things that are asked of you, you continue to be loved by your Savior and receive his blessings, though you do not deserve even one. Christ's abundant grace should be most reassuring to you because it means you are not required to merit his favor. Indeed, you cannot earn your salvation. Instead, grace is an unmerited gift of divine favor that first results in your salvation and then continues to operate in you to bring about the righteous nature that God desires in you.

Friend, grace is getting what you don't deserve and not getting what you do deserve. It is grace that saved you, grace that sustains you, and grace that keeps you from falling. You nor I would be saved if grace were not undeserved favor and were it not a constant in the heart and nature of God. More than this, as though salvation alone is not enough, grace is also the holy influence that works within you to change your prideful thoughts of merit after achievement to thoughts of thanksgiving and praise for what you have received, that you have been saved for an eternal life where you will enjoy infinitely more than you deserve. Think on this, and often, for your right relationship with God depends on you seeing grace for what it is, a priceless gift from him. I pray your awareness and appreciation of grace will stir up gratitude and obedience, resulting in a life that brings increasing pleasure and glory to the Lord. Amen.

For God did not send His Son
into the world to condemn the world,
but that the world through Him might be saved.

JOHN 3:17

And not only that, but we also rejoice in
God through our Lord Jesus Christ,
through whom we have now received the reconciliation.

ROMANS 5:11

For He made Him who knew no sin to be sin for us,
that we might become the righteousness of God in Him.

2 CORINTHIANS 5:21

And He Himself is the propitiation for our sins,
and not for ours only but also for the whole world.

1 JOHN 2:2

Atonement and Redemption

BELOVED, WE SINNERS owe a moral debt to a holy and just God because we disobey his commands daily. We cannot of ourselves ever pay this moral debt because it requires something we do not have to offer: a blameless life free of sin. Jesus, however, sinless and without blame, paid this moral debt on our behalf by offering his perfect life on the cross as a ransom for our souls. This glorious act of perfect sacrifice was the atonement, the making right of a great wrong, that is, the created sinning against the Creator. Christ's death satisfied our moral debt to God forever and always and redeemed (freed) us from condemnation and eternal death. You are redeemed by the atoning work of Christ. Friend, praise God! You have been delivered from sin and unto an eternal heavenly life!

Christ died for all, and they who believe are saved. Christ, suffering until death on the cross, made the atonement for all mankind, effecting your redemption. But where the atonement was an event that took place "once for all," redemption is constantly taking place within the hearts of all of God's people, including you. Because you are forgiven and are under God's grace, you are no longer a slave to sin. Yet, you remain imperfect; therefore, sin will continue to tempt you in all its power and effect. You must resist this temptation. Guard yourself against thinking and behaving as if you claim the benefits of atonement but do not see the need to honor it with a reformed life. If you truly believe your life is saved through Jesus Christ, then your life must leave your old ways and move in the direction of God's will.

Friend, I beg you not to consider yourself beyond forgiveness. I once was of this mind, and I realize now it is a very arrogant thing to think. My sins are more powerful than the atoning power of Jesus' sacrifice? Certainly not! Let us not think such foolish thoughts, for it is precisely what the evil one wants us to believe so that we might become doubters and unwittingly invite him to use us for his wicked ways. Not one of us, not even you or me, have sinned so much that we cannot be forgiven and saved. Your redemption is secure when you genuinely believe in the Lord and the efficacy of his blood, which was shed for thee.

By God's generous grace, you have never been any more redeemed or free than you are today, and this truth shall remain the truth forever more. Amen.

And I will pray to the Father, and He
will give you another Helper,
that He may abide with you forever— the Spirit of truth,
whom the world cannot receive, because it
neither sees Him nor knows Him;
but you know Him, for He dwells
with you and will be in you.

JOHN 14:16-17

And when they had prayed,
the place where they were assembled together was shaken;
and they were all filled with the Holy Spirit,
and they spoke the word of God with boldness.

ACTS 4:31

Holy Spirit

FRIEND, I HAVE shared good news with you in my previous letters. Indulge me while I teach you a little more. As I've told you, you cannot fix yourself. Consequently, you might be afraid that you will experience failure at Christian living because it seems such an unlikely way to live, even if you believe in everything you have learned thus far. Well, I have more good news. Jesus told the apostles he was sending an "advocate" to be their helper. That advocate, the Holy Spirit, would help them carry out their assignment. The Holy Spirit is, thanks be to God, with you now and desires to help you as well.

The Father and the Son and the Holy Spirit, the Triune God, are equal and work in harmony with one another. The three persons of the Trinity are intimately related, mutually indwelling one another and sharing the divine essence. The Father is the creator; he chooses, plans, and wills. The Son is the fulfiller; he obeys the Father and does His will. The Spirit dwells in us, pointing us to the Father and the Son. The uniqueness of the Holy Spirit is his loving and influential living presence within you on a day-to-day basis. Jesus promised that the Holy Spirit would live within each of us who believe. Your indwelling advocate empowers you to live victoriously for the cause of Christ and the glory of God. You need the Holy Spirit as a facilitator to become who God created you to be, and through his power, you have divine assistance in all situations. Tempted by sin? Call on the Holy Spirit. Burdened with fear? Call on the Holy Spirit. Struggling to demonstrate the attributes of Christian living? Call on the Holy Spirit!

Praise the Lord, for the Holy Spirit lives within you, changing your heart, giving you increasing faith, and transforming your life. In the Old Testament, God was so glorious that no one could approach him. Today, because of grace and the great blessing of atonement and redemption, God the Father and God the Son dwell in you through the presence of the Holy Spirit.

Friend, if you were to heartfully commit yourself to following the example of Jesus Christ, the Holy Spirit will assure your success. Your advocate will help you tune into the voice of God and, in faith, follow through with whatever you believe he is calling you to. The

Holy Spirit will help you in practical ways, giving you insight into what you read in the Bible and helping you recall what you have learned through the scriptures. He brings to your mind understanding and truth. He empowers you with wisdom and compassion and the ability to respond as Jesus would to the circumstances of your life.

The fact that God is Triune – three persons in eternal relationship – should remind you that relationships are what life is meant to be about. Life is not about power, possessions, or success. It's about thriving in loving relationships, especially with the Lord. May it be so for you and yours, forever and ever. Amen

For God so loved the world that He
gave His only begotten Son,
that whoever believes in Him should not
perish but have everlasting life.

JOHN 3:16

Most assuredly, I say to you,
he who believes in Me has everlasting life.

JOHN 6:47

Believe

FRIEND, IT CAN be easy to let doubts and reservations creep in and cause your belief to waver. You might ask how you can believe what you cannot see. Indeed, I asked this question myself before I believed. Today, I understand that such a question assumes that God should be reducible to our human level of understanding. You must not attempt to reduce the nonreducible; you cannot comprehend the ways of God. You must worship him by faith rather than evidence. Do we want our God to be easily comprehended within the limitations of our simple reasoning abilities? Do we want our God to be that small? How, then, could we be in awe of him if we could rationally understand his ways? It is better, isn't it, to worship a God who is incomprehensible on a scale so grand that he is far beyond the precise understanding of those who worship him?

Now, be still and consider the origin of the intricate

design of a rosebud just before it blooms, the beauty of the constellations set against a dark night sky, and how the birds know that it is morning before the sun rises. Creation and all other miracles are the evidence of God's existence shown to you so that you might more easily believe in him. Yet, those who believe without seeing are even more blessed, for they walk by faith instead of sight. Increase your belief without evidence but instead with trusting faith, and you will grow more intimate with the Lord. If your belief should wane, and it most likely will from time to time, rush to kneel and pray that it will swiftly increase! God loves those who earnestly seek him; your prayer for increased belief will most certainly be answered.

Moreover, believe in Christ and his resurrection, too, for that also pleases God. It is through the sufferings of Christ that you are enabled to come to God. Without Christ and his death on the cross, there would be no reconciliation with God. You are reconciled with God when you believe in the atoning work of his Son. The Father promises if you believe and trust in Christ, his Son, he will give you this eternal life you hear me speak of. Believe that what lies ahead for believers is far greater than anything that has or will come to pass in the present world. This is the promise of God to those who believe in the saving grace of his Son: you will see a new Heaven and a new Earth and live an eternal life with a heavenly inheritance, affording you more joy than you can now imagine.

Your belief in God and His teachings is essential to establishing your faith. I encourage you to read and study the Bible to increase your belief in God the Father and Christ your Savior. By reading and studying the Bible, you will gain a deeper understanding of God's Word and His teachings. I also encourage you to pray. By talking to God in prayer, you can express your most troubling thoughts, feelings, and doubts to him, and in doing so, you will strengthen your relationship with him. And I encourage you to attend church and fellowship with other believers so that you may gain encouragement and support as you seek to increase your belief.

Please always remember that living a Christian life is a long journey that takes time, effort, and practice to strengthen and deepen your commitment to God. Do not tire of this worthy pursuit. I assure you that by incorporating the disciplines of Bible study, prayer, and worship into your routine, you will experience an increase in your belief in God and his ways.

Friend, please push yourself beyond simply believing in God—believe God. Your belief in God, Christ, and the Holy Spirit and their love for you will remind you and bind you to your purpose. There is no better reassurance than to believe God. Even Christ said, "Just believe." For you, I pray that your belief in our holy God and all his divine attributes will increase in abundance each day. May it be so!

Meditate on these things; give yourself entirely to them,
that your progress may be evident to all.

1 TIMOTHY 4:15

Meaning

YOU UNDERSTAND YOUR purpose, and you know that you must believe. Now, one day, you will feel drawn to give meaning to your life. All creatures desire significance in their existence; we want to believe we made a difference in the world and left something worthy behind so that others will remember us. Resist the temptation to find meaning in worldly pursuits, no matter how worthy they may seem. Resist the temptation to congratulate yourself or boast of your talent or wisdom as you experience new accomplishments. Be sure of your motives in all that you do and give yourself to. You are not forbidden from being righteous before men but from making it your goal to be seen as righteous for the sake of receiving their praise. The world and its expectations are fickle, and you will never be satisfied if you think your life's meaning is to be found in praise from men.

Instead, find your meaning in serving God. Do not find meaning in anything you have done in the past, or expect more meaning to be found in what you plan to do in the future. For yesterday is gone, and tomorrow may never come. Live as if today were your last day, surrendering every aspect of your life to God, seeking to live more and more as Christ lived, even in your final moments. Your meaning, in fact, your satisfaction in life will be found in your earnest pursuit of serving the God who created you.

The true meaning of life is to know and obey God as your Creator, to enjoy the rest of God's creation, and to reflect his character so that others may see some of the beauty of God as you know and experience him in Christ. The hope you have in Christ should be the source of your greatest joy. As God's child, you have a glorious hope of eternal life, a hope not only of eternal existence but that you become a joint heir with Christ. Let your meaning be defined by a heavenly inheritance that is yet to come but is as sure to come as the sun rises on every new day.

Again, find your meaning in your relationship with God. Praise God and enjoy the blessings he has put before you today. Always remember there is meaning in every breath you draw because you are a representative of Christ, and your actions should give meaning to what he has done for you. God gives you meaning, and that meaning should drive you to fulfill your only purpose, and to remind you, that is to glorify him. Look for meaning elsewhere, and it will indeed be very difficult for you to achieve your purpose. What is life without your divine purpose?

Child of God, let your existential quest for meaning begin and end with God. There is meaning in knowing and sharing the Gospel. Be an effective and productive child of God, commit yourself to the meaning you have in Christ, and refuse to let anyone lead you astray. Be a beacon of light and shine brightly so others can see what you do for your Lord. May your meaning in Christ always guide you into righteousness. Amen.

Beloved, let us love one another, for love is of God;
and everyone who loves is born of God and knows God.
He who does not love does not know God, for God is love.

1 JOHN 4:7-8

Love

OH, FRIEND, HOW much I love you as a companion in Christ! I love others as well, and so too must you. Take joy in those you love. But remember, where it is easy to love the loveable, it is more righteous to love the difficult to love. True love is more than tender feelings and emotional rewards; it is a decision. Yes, it is a decision to love even when it is difficult to do so. You should make up your mind to love regardless of your feelings. Only then can your love become greater for another than it is for yourself. Above all, love God no matter what you must endure in the world. The knowledge that God loves you beyond measure and does so unconditionally should compel you to go into the world to love others in the same way.

Take great care not to befriend only those who are advantageous to you. Christ died not only for his friends but his enemies as well because he loved them so much. By loving *all* others, you continue Christ's work of sharing grace and the hope of everlasting life. By loving all others, it is easy to pray that everyone would know Jesus and be bound for Heaven. Remember, Jesus dined with and cared for the outcast instead of limiting himself only to the company of great men. You should do the same.

You cannot profess to follow Christ unless you love all those for whom Christ died. We were instructed to love our neighbor as we love ourselves. Love others so well that there will be kindness and mutual acts of service between you. You may commit acts of charity and kindness, but unless your acts are motivated by love, your good deeds mean nothing in the eyes of the Lord. It is in your love for your neighbor that you continue Christ's work of spreading the hope of salvation and everlasting life. All relationships are made perfect if filled with love but are worthless without it. Love everyone without hesitation, all for God's greater glory, and much love will be returned to you.

God willing, one day, you may be a parent. Unreasonable scolding, hurtful language, or cruel punishment brings about resentment in children, making you ineffective in the Christian training of children. Love them as Jesus loved them — with patience, kindness, protection, trust, and hope, always keeping them from becoming discouraged. This is the way in which your Lord loves you; follow his example. Treat the little ones with generous love.

Lastly, Christ suffered the punishment of our sins so that we might be reconciled with God. All he asks in return is that we obey the new law: to love one another. Love is compassionate and kind, not harmful. Don't let the fact that you were treated wrongly cause you to commit another wrong. Instead, overcome evil with love, mercy, and restraint. May you always love with abandon, for you will always be loved in never-ending abundance. Amen.

The Lord is near to all who call upon Him,
to all who call upon Him in truth.
He will fulfill the desire of those who fear Him;
he also will hear their cry and save them.

PSALM 145:18-19

Prayer

MY FRIEND, REMEMBER the times we kneeled to pray. We pray because we believe our Father listens. Prayer is the way in which the life of a Christian is nourished. Talk with God, be yourself before him, and let him commune with you. Let your prayers be a daily habit. Let them be simple in nature and rooted in your heart. Too much thinking about your prayers will only lead you to produce clanging sounds that are harsh in God's ears. Don't try to impress him with refined words, memorized verses, and eloquent recitations. Just be you. Just tell him what worries you. Tell him what you need. Ask that his will be done and then be satisfied that he heard you and will respond in due time. Remember, his timing is divine, and yours is not, so it should not be a surprise to you if he does not give you precisely what you want when you want it. When that is the case, be patient. Often, what is refined in you while you are waiting is the best answer to your prayers.

In Jesus Christ, go boldly to God with your prayers. And do not simply pray for favor and things, but pray for others. Pray that you and those you love will be drawn closer to God, and pray for unpleasant circumstances to change so that God's glory may shine through. Remember that while on the cross, Jesus prayed for his enemies; he was clear about his desire and command that we, too, should pray for others as he did. What more extraordinary display of love for your neighbor and brother is there than to bow and pray for him? It pleases the Lord when we pray for others, so do so often. Very often.

In prayer is the best way to spend time alone with God. It is when you are alone with him that you are free from distraction and temptation to impress with your actions and words. There are times for public and corporate prayer, and there are times for private prayer. Kneel often and be sincere with your Lord. Make private time with him so that you can go before him and speak without hesitation or shame about what you need or what hurts you the most.

Friend, pray continually, on all occasions, and with all kinds of prayers and requests, for the Lord is faithful. And as you draw nearer to him, he will strengthen and protect you, growing you in righteousness and enriching you with blessings. Daily prayer strengthens your walk with Christ, increasing your endurance for his sake. Pray kneeling, standing, as you sink into your pillow, and even when driving or pushing a grocery cart. Your prayer ritual is unimportant; it is that you pray often and with sincerity that matters most. Most of all, pray with thanksgiving, for you should always be thankful that you can speak directly to God. Amen.

Now faith is the substance of things hoped for,
the evidence of things not seen.

Hebrews 11:1

Faith

WHAT IS FAITH? Faith is an invisible thing. Christians live by faith, not by sight. Faith is not simply an emotion or thought process but is an unwavering confidence built on the knowledge and belief that God is who he says he is. Faith is throwing yourself with abandon at the foot of the cross and believing everything remarkable that was accomplished there. Friend, if your faith is dependent on what you can see and understand, it is built on a very weak foundation. You might think it unreal if you can't see it, smell it, taste it, or touch it. But if you have true faith, you can sense it. What does it feel like? It feels like the complete absence of worry and the reassuring fullness of the comfort of peace. Faith feels like this because, as a believer, you know that death is not your end; instead, it is your transition to being in the presence of God. Those who believe in what they cannot see shall inherit an everlasting life. This is why it is so important that you have faith!

Faith is believing that God loves you and will provide for you and fulfill all the promises he has made to you. When you stop counting on yourself and begin to believe God is in control of all things, you will have arrived at that blessed place of surrender where you will experience an immeasurable calm, even relief from the weight of worldly burdens and cares. Have faith enough to trust yourself completely in the hands of God, follow him wherever he may lead, and your steps will be sure for they will be guided by your faith in his goodness.

Do not be discouraged if your faith falters. Diminished faith does not mean that you have lost your faith, only that you are undergoing a trial that challenges your beliefs. Perhaps you think a prayer has not been answered, or your heart has been shattered with bitter disappointment, or worse, a painful loss. Do not think God is punishing you; he is not. He weeps with you. You live in a broken world that cannot provide for you what can only be found in Heaven. Expect brokenness in a broken world, and pain in brokenness. These are the times when you need God's comfort most. Trust him to lead you through the brokenness and believe that there is no disappointment in your heavenly home. Without faith it is impossible to have a right relationship with God, so ask him to increase your faith during all challenging times, and he will do it.

Friend, do not forget that faith is meant to be shared with others. You must make your thankful thoughts and sensation of inner peace known through speaking of it to others. The business of the church is not only to save but to enlighten. Christ is the light, and his disciples must also be light. It is not a life of good works, but one work that is required, and that is to have a faith that would enable you to rely on Christ and, from such faith, to lead a Christ-like life. To fit in with the crowd is to miss an opportunity to be an example of Jesus and show his goodness and mercy to anyone watching you. Always reveal your faith in Christ with your words as well as your good and selfless deeds. May your faith increase with each new day! Amen.

Obey and you will be blessed.
Disobey and you will be cursed.

DEUTERONOMY 11:26–28

So if you walk in My ways,
to keep My statutes and My commandments,
as your father David walked,
then I will lengthen your days.

1 KINGS 3:14

Submit to God and be at peace with him;
in this way prosperity will come to you.
Accept instruction from his mouth
and lay up his words in your heart.

JOB 22:21-22

If you keep My commandments,
you will abide in My love,
just as I have kept My Father's
commandments and abide in His love.

JOHN 15:10

Obedience

FRIEND, A TRAIT we have in common is our desire to choose our own way, to be the director of the movie in which we are the star. But to obey God, we must step down from the director's chair and permit him to take his rightful place in our lives as our sovereign Lord. Let us encourage one another in this way. We must strive to faithfully obey the Lord. I know that submission to authority is contrary to your nature. Nonetheless, submission is required of you, and for a very good reason. Your outward obedience to Christian precepts is proof to the world of your trust in Jesus, and your inward strivings to please the Lord in all you do is the beginning of discovering God's will for your life.

Your outward obedience to Christian precepts is going to be a much easier task for you. God's precepts are well-known in the Word and firmly established in the traditions of the church. You will find your open display of obedience less challenging as you spend time in the Word and permit Scripture to inform and motivate you. Fellowship with other Christians furthers your compliance, as good company begets good conduct in you. Christian obedience is the act of submitting to the will of God, your Creator, and your highest authority. If you have faith, obedience should become the daily practice of living by faith, obeying the teachings of the Bible, believing they are the guidestones that lead you to a more fulfilling life. To be truly obedient, you must remain in a proper relationship with Christ, acknowledging him as your Savior through grace alone — that you did nothing of merit sufficient to save yourself. Faith in Christ and gratitude for what he accomplished for you produces the power that leads to obedience. And this power is also not of yourself, but of the Holy Spirit, the helper Jesus promised for each of us. The more you strive to be obedient, the more your life becomes guided by the Holy Spirit. As your helper, he will not lead you astray. If you are willing to trust and obey God and try to live a holy life, he will reveal himself to you and direct your steps through the prompting of the Holy Spirit. This is the second form of obedience that is required of you, submission to God's private and unique conversations delivered directly to you. You may call it your conscience, but I believe it is the Holy Spirit prompting you to discern God's will for you, and then urging you to obey.

Living in obedience to God in all things, even the seemingly inconsequential details of day-to-day living, reveals your love and respect for him. Obedience is actually in itself a form of worship, acknowledging who God is and accepting your responsibility in relation to him. Remember, too, that every command God will make of you isn't always only for his sake but for yours as well. The call to obedience is for your benefit because he knows what is best for you.

Through his sacrifice on the cross, Jesus took away our just punishment and laid a new obligation to obedience upon us. All he asks in return is that we obey the new law: to love one another. That grace has taken the place of the old law does not mean that disobedience has replaced obedience. If we accept Jesus as our Savior, we must also accept him as our King to rule over us and, in doing so, reveal the moral characteristic of the life of Christ thriving within us. A disobedient life shows there is neither gratitude nor humility within you.

Friend, do not take salvation for granted and act as though you are unchanged. Train yourself to be godly, obey the Word, and rise above your nature, demonstrating your renewal so that others may wish to follow your example. Obedience to God is the sign of your sheer delight and joyful thankfulness for your salvation. You are to rid yourself of your former way of life and put on a new self, one created to be like God in true righteousness and holiness. Do not live the rest of your life for unholy desires, but rather for the will of God. If you are guided by the Holy Spirit, you will not obey the lusts of the flesh and temptations of evil. Act like Jesus and find yourself satisfied in higher and long-lasting ways.

To live by faith includes the discipline of prayer, commonly going to God in thanksgiving and requests. When you know that you are struggling to become or remain obedient, pray for guidance and inspiration; ask for self-control so that you may obey rather than rebel. Prayer itself is a form of obedience, for Scripture tells you to humble yourself and pray. And when a righteous person, a true believer committed to Christ, by his striving to live for God with increasing obedience presents a fervent prayer, it avails much.

The more you depend on God, the more obedient you must be. He loves you and wants only what is best for you. And when you love him in return and walk faithfully with him, obeying from the heart all his commandments, good blessing will indeed come to you. Love God, your Father, your Christ, and your Helper; and obey him with a thankful heart. Amen.

For My thoughts are not your thoughts,
nor are your ways My ways, says the Lord.
For as the heavens are higher than the earth,
so are My ways higher than your ways,
and My thoughts than your thoughts.

ISAIAH 55:8-9

If any of you lacks wisdom, let him ask of God,
who gives to all liberally and without reproach,
and it will be given to him.

JAMES 1:5

Knowledge and Wisdom

KNOWLEDGE IS ITS own temptation, so do not seek knowledge only to lift yourself up. Too much reasoning is a great hindrance to the nurturing of a spiritual life, for it always leads to pride in oneself. It is far better to feed spiritual hunger than intellectual curiosity. God tells us to be still and know that he is God. He teaches us that with much human wisdom comes much sorrow, and with more worldly knowledge, more grief. Christ tells us we are to receive the kingdom of God like a little child, with wide-eyed wonder, joy, and gratitude. This is true wisdom. It is wise to trust God and enjoy your life as he unfolds it for you than to pursue wisdom for selfish gain, especially if your hope is to add to your life anything other than more of God. It is better to reason less and be happy and do good while we are alive, for you cannot know the number of your days. You cannot add an hour to your life with human knowledge and wisdom.

Yet, righteous wisdom is a valuable trait that is highly prized in the Christian faith. It is the ability to understand and apply righteous knowledge in a way that benefits yourself and others. Righteous wisdom is more valuable than any material possession. It will guide you to make good decisions and live a fulfilling life. Righteous wisdom comes from God; through studying the Bible, seeking guidance in prayer, and seeking the advice of spiritually mature people, we gain righteous wisdom. Ask God for his wisdom in any situation, and he will provide it to you.

Take great care that your wisdom is not boastful. No matter your well-meaning, if your wisdom is laced with bragging, whether about your intellectual accomplishments in this world or your own superior morality, no one will happily listen. All ears become shut off to you because no one wants to be an audience to your uprightness and self-righteousness. You must always take a humble position in every situation and only share wisdom as a lowly one grateful to have learned a necessary lesson. Only then can you give credit to God for the heavenly knowledge and wisdom with which he has blessed you.

Always remember that the foolishness of God is wiser than your wisdom, and the weakness of God is stronger than your strength. If you rely on your own wisdom in all things, you fail to seek the will of God. If you seek the will of God, you will have divine wisdom in your thinking and peace in your heart. In all matters, ask Christ to go with you and bless you in what you are about to undertake.

I remind you that God says to be still. There is a reason for this instruction. Heavenly knowledge and wisdom are the products of insightful reflection. Pause, number your blessings, consider what the Lord has done for you in both a temporal and eternal perspective, and become wise in the ways he would have you live. Child of God, examine your thoughts, words, and deeds often, and take the necessary steps to align yourself in a proper relationship with Christ. Do not compare yourself to what others are able to articulate or do, but instead strive to please God alone in all that you do. This is the wisdom that matters.

Yes, my friend, humble and unassuming wisdom will allow you to make good decisions, live a fulfilling life, understand the world and people around you, and, more importantly, know the will of God for your life. It is something that, if nourished properly, is constantly developing, and it is a character trait that you should hope to acquire. It is indeed the highest wisdom to want and try to live according to the will of God. I pray for you that this is the wisdom you desire. May it be so!

When pride comes, then comes shame;
but with the humble is wisdom.

PROVERBS 11:2

For we dare not class ourselves or compare ourselves
with those who commend themselves.
But they, measuring themselves by themselves,
and comparing themselves among
themselves, are not wise.

2 CORINTHIANS 10:12

God resists the proud,
but gives grace to the humble.

JAMES 4:6

Pride and Humility

DEAR FRIEND, ONE who is so loved and treasured, I know it would be easy for you to think too much of yourself. You are not alone; I wrestle with this shortcoming as well. Indeed, humility is not an easy sign of character to develop. It is a hard thing to master, but master it you must. To be humble is good in every situation. God does not want us to think too highly of ourselves. Instead, he wants us to think lowly and soundly of ourselves. The reason for this is he wants you to accept that humility is the right understanding of who you are before himself. Your humility before God is where you must start in your endeavors to develop this important trademark of a believer. You need to be humble before God and dependent on him, always seeking his will. To be humble before God means to recognize that you are not self-sufficient; rather, you depend on God for all that you need. All you have comes from him, for you can create nothing for yourself. I hope that by now this fact is well established in your understanding.

No one is perfect, not me, not even you. The pursuit of perfection is a tool the enemy uses to reduce you to a state of self-pity. When you focus on what you don't have, you fail to recognize what you do have. When you are more occupied with achieving perfection than with appreciating how you have already been blessed, short-comings, imperfections, and all, you may blame God for your circumstances rather than thank him as you should. God knows your defects and why he gave them to you. He did so that you would find peace in him, not the world nor in yourself, so that his glory would shine through in you just as he made you. Do not let yourself get caught up with thoughts that you need more, or that you must be more. Be satisfied in the perfection of Jesus's love for you and the way in which God designed you. And thus satisfied, be bighearted and accepting of the weaknesses and imperfections of others.

Remember that true humility compels you to look after the interests of others before looking after your own interests. Humility never threatens, insults, or ridicules. Humility produces in you a kind and unas-suming spirit, which is easy for others to befriend. Humility is not a weakness but a quiet strength rooted in self-control and deference. The goal of humility is not so much self-denial as it is self-restraint so that others might be lifted up and encouraged.

When pride and conceit arise within you, look quickly to Jesus for your example. Although he was from the highest place, Jesus spent time with the lowest of the low, showing that his mercy and grace are for all. Let there be harmony and a spirit of agreement wherever you go, for the way to secure grace more abundantly is to be humble before the Lord. Be humble with others, just as Jesus is with you. Swallow your pride and do not point out your humble nature, for even that would be to brag. Every hint of pride must be cast aside. Always be humble, looking to the interests of others, and you will abound in loving, wholesome friendship with everyone.

I heard of a man who claimed to have disciplined himself so well that he had achieved a life without sin. I suppose he had forgotten that self-righteousness is a deadly form of pride and among the worst sins. I pray that your heart would fill with humility, and that you would love and honor God in a meek and grateful spirit. Amen.

When He had called the people to Himself,
with His disciples also, He said to them,
"Whoever desires to come after Me, let him deny himself,
and take up his cross, and follow Me."

MARK 8:34

Therefore submit to God. Resist the devil
and he will flee from you.

JAMES 4:7

Therefore humble yourselves under
the mighty hand of God,
that He may exalt you in due time.

1 PETER 5:6

Surrender

I URGE YOU to surrender your will, your knowledge, your reason, your experience, your motives, your time, your treasure, your plans, your future, your desires, your comfort — your everything — to God. And not simply to God, but to God and his ways, his purpose, and his desire to bring you into a right relationship with himself. This is a challenging request, to be sure, but God is sovereign, and you are not. There is absolutely nothing that happens in the universe that is outside of God's influence and authority. As King of kings and Lord of lords, God has no limitations. The sovereignty of God is not merely that God has the power and right to govern all things, including his creation, man (you), but that he does govern all things, always and without exception, in your life as well as in mine. Surrender to his authority, and all will be well for you.

Friend, do not love the world and its temporary

distractions. Learn to be disinterested in the world and what it expects of you and concentrate instead on God. Love him more than yourself and his glory more than approval and praise for yourself. This requires you to hold his will in higher regard than your own. Nothing about the world can be enjoyed in its proper perspective until you lay down your will and surrender yourself completely to God. To surrender is to accept whatever God sends and do nothing to try to change it. Do not allow pride and ambition to keep you from becoming who God, in his mercy, designed you to be. Do not trust your own power or knowledge. Your aim should not be greatness but humility, to surrender completely, to become lowly rather than haughty in spirit, to be concerned only with how to glorify God.

Beloved, this is the confidence you have in approaching God: that if you ask for anything according to his will, he hears you. Submit yourself, then, to God. Come near to him, and he will come near to you. Do not be foolish, but understand and remember what the Lord's will is, that you turn away from your own will, which, being of the flesh, will always lead you astray.

God graciously provided you and me with Jesus as the cure for our sins. It is best that you place complete confidence in him as your means for partaking in the eternal life to come, that blessed fellowship with God. Remember that God did not send his Son into the world to judge the world guilty, but to save the world through his willing sacrifice. Christ is the gift, which is sufficient evidence of God's love for you. Submit yourself to Christ, then, and believe in his power to restore you to a right relationship with God. He who believes in the Son is not condemned. Those who believe in Jesus will receive God's special love, and they shall never perish but shall be saved with everlasting salvation. It is good for you in every way to accept this truth, and surrender all, once and for all, to God, your Creator, and Jesus, your Savior.

I know it sounds odd to forego your own will, to lay your plans aside and rid yourself of all hunger for power and control. You will struggle over and over again to surrender completely, just as I do. But I promise you, the more you seek God's will rather than your own, the better your life will be. I pray you learn to yield and that you do so with a joyful heart. May it be so!

*But those who desire to be rich fall
into temptation and a snare,
and into many foolish and harmful lusts
which drown men in destruction and perdition.*

1 Timothy 6:9

*Do not love the world or the things in the world.
If anyone loves the world, the love
of the Father is not in him.
For all that is in the world—the lust
of the flesh, the lust of the eyes,
and the pride of life—is not of the
Father but is of the world.
And the world is passing away, and the lust of it;
but he who does the will of God abides forever.*

1 John 2:15-17

Simplicity

FRIEND, DO NOT overcomplicate your life. Avoid letting your mind become preoccupied with your circumstances, as this hinders your understanding of the will of God. Complications steal joy and bring frustration. A simple Christian life is a surrendered life — a life where temporary worldly pleasures have no power and hold over you but rather can be set aside in favor of rest, worship, and acts of service. Such simplicity offers moments for quiet meditation in which God may reveal himself to you. You are called to live a simple life, free from the distractions and excesses of the world. Only then will your focus be on God and his kingdom.

Please understand that the great enemy of simplicity is a hunger for this world. The Christian is the person to whom his relationship with God through Christ is his greatest love. If instead, you set your heart on having earthly possessions, uninterrupted happiness, constant pleasure, and luxurious comfort, you are quite vulnerable, for you might lose these temporary things at any moment. Such a person can easily be disappointed and desperately hurt. On the other hand, if you give to Jesus Christ the highest place of honor in your life, you are right with God, and nothing on Earth can take that away from you.

The life I wish for you is not a life where you relentlessly deny yourself of things that might bring you comfort and pleasure. Instead, I wish for you to live a life focused on what is truly important, not distracted or tempted by things that are of no eternal value. A simple Christian life is letting go of everything that might hinder your walk with God and opening your heart and mind to embrace God as your greatest treasure, freeing yourself to live a life of willful commitment and humble obedience to him. The pursuit of things, power, reputation, and applause will only hinder the enjoyment of a simple life centered on God.

Living a simple life will also enable you to be more in tune with the needs of others. When you simplify your life, and when you are less preoccupied with what you must do to maintain your complicated life, you become better able to see and respond to the needs of others. When living a simple life, you will become more open to serving others and living out the teachings of Jesus Christ. I assure you, busyness will rob you of this great pleasure. Remember, too, that a simple life is a less stressful life, and that is good for everyone you love.

I pray that you be blessed with the discernment to know what to deal with and what to leave alone, what to pursue and what not to pursue. May you learn to live each moment in his presence, giving yourself completely to him and the plans he has for you. May he be pleased with each and every day of your life as you learn to be satisfied with your daily bread, serving as an example to others that wealth, possessions, busyness, and constant striving do not always result in joy. Be content with leading a simple life. May it be so!

And let us not grow weary while doing good,
for in due season we shall reap if we do not lose heart.

GALATIANS 6:9

For this is commendable, if because
of conscience toward God
one endures grief, suffering wrongfully.
For what credit is it if,
when you are beaten for your faults, you take it patiently?
But when you do good and suffer, if you take it patiently,
this is commendable before God.

1 PETER 2:19–20

Endurance

LIFE IS FULL of joy, but it includes pain and consequences, too. Remember that you are not yet in Heaven where all is perfect; rather, you are living in a broken world where trials and disappointment abound. Therefore, it is important that you understand that in this life, you are not destined for happiness or health but for holiness. Accept the consequences as they come without any complaints. Don't wallow in self-pity. Instead, look to God to help you endure the pain and consequences of life while in this temporary, less-than-perfect world. Let God separate you from every affection and desire not grounded in him and his glory. After you have endured a few trials while trusting in the Lord, trials will trouble you less and less. You will have realized that God is more than enough.

How do you keep on going along the path of obedience to Christ, you might ask; how do you keep going month after month for years or decades when there are countless disappointments, obstacles, betrayals, and failures, even grief, in your journey? If you put your hope in the sovereign grace and power of God and not in your own strength, or in the approval of others, or in fleeting pleasures, or the praise of mere men, you will endure anything as your faith remains steadfast in Christ. He will not require anything of you for which he does not provide the necessary wisdom, strength, and guidance for your eventual victory. Because he is faithful, you must be faithful; you must endure hardship and keep your heart and mind open to his leading.

It is a painful and difficult lesson, but you must learn to take for good whatever God sends in your direction, however bitter to the taste and painful to the heart and bones it may be. He is trying to teach you something or is using you to teach something to someone else (it is a great honor to be used in such a way). Both are his praiseworthy prerogatives; submit to either objective. You know that all around you there are signs of evil and subversions of the truth. You must stand firm and look beyond these things to the Lord Jesus Christ. In the face of long-suffering or an experience of evil perpetrated against you, stick to your belief, a belief anchored not on the philosophy or opinions of man, but on the promises of God and his offer of salvation and delivery through the atoning work of Jesus Christ. The promises of God will help you to endure whatever may come.

Please remember this — in stubbornness, you refuse the Lord, but in submissiveness, you trust in him who is merciful and just. Do not love the world and its fickle promises and make your guilt and condemnation greater. But turn away from the world and its unholy allure and murmurs that your life is unfair and go to Christ with a broken and remorseful spirit, and you will be gladly received and restored.

Please be assured that God is not unjust; he will not forget your good deeds and the love you show him as you help your neighbors to endure as well. Continue in your enduring love of the Lord and service to your neighbors, demonstrating for others who suffer that they, too, may lay hold of the full assurance of hope found in Christ. I pray that your trials be few in number, that you endure them well, and you be reassured knowing a heavenly home without disappointments is your reward for what you may endure today. Amen.

A fool's wrath is known at once,
but a prudent man covers shame.

PROVERBS 12:16

He who is slow to anger is better than the mighty,
and he who rules his spirit than he who takes a city.

PROVERBS 16:32

A fool vents all his feelings,
but a wise man holds them back.

PROVERBS 29:11

Self-Control

CHILD OF GOD, you cannot simply dismiss your bad behavior by saying, "That's just how I am." To do that is to be unapologetic for the hurt or embarrassment you may cause to others. May self-control be one of your defining traits. Self-control not only of your temper, but also your tongue. Be careful not to act or speak rashly, especially in anger. Under the influence of anger, you will be tempted to display conduct very different from God's righteousness. If Christ is in you, then so too must be self-control.

You may not believe me at first, but you are able to control yourself. Self-control is a fruit of the spirit, a gift within each of us, but one that must be mastered. To master self-control, you must be aware of how you feel and think about what is on your mind. You must consider what the outcome will be if you were to express your raw emotions, say what is on your mind, or continue to think about someone with malice in your heart. If the outcome is likely something that God would condemn, put an immediate stop to the thoughts or feelings that are leading you astray.

Whenever you have doubts about whatever you are doing or considering, stop it immediately. Your doubt is the Holy Spirit reminding you to do only what is right in the sight of God. If you are about to choose what is not pleasing to him, he will give you a sense of restraint, one which you must heed. Stay alert; keep your senses sharp before God. The body is weak; guard against its temptation with prayer, relying on God's strength and giving him praise for his power to bless you with self-control.

Self-indulgence disgraces the Lord, for it was his self-sacrifice that gave you the promise of life. It also discourages other Christians who may be weak in their faith and look to you as an encourager. Pursue what is right and acknowledge Christ with your unselfish conduct. If you know how to do the right thing and choose not to, your sin is greater because of your knowledge. But if you conquer temptation and give yourself entirely to God, he will work mightily in you. Be aware of temptation at all times, and always deny yourself selfish or dishonest gains.

Please, do not think yourself able to resist temptation

and carelessly expose yourself to it. One cannot both indulge in the deeds of darkness and wear the armor of light. Light represents truth, knowledge, and holiness. Darkness represents ignorance, error, falsehood, and sin. Darkness will keep you from being a productive Christian. Unholy behavior thrives in darkness, but the children of God need no hiding place. Love the Lord and let his light shine through you as you master your thoughts and actions. May you never lose an opportunity to represent Christ well because of your lack of self-control. Amen!

Blessed be the God and Father of our Lord Jesus Christ,
the Father of mercies and God of all comfort,
who comforts us in all our tribulation,
that we may be able to comfort those
who are in any trouble,
with the comfort with which we
ourselves are comforted by God.

2 CORINTHIANS 1:3-4

Trials and Suffering

I MUST TELL you, there will be trials and suffering throughout your life, but take courage, for God is with you! Life includes pain and disappointment, so we must learn to bear with and endure suffering with expectancy and patience. Much suffering will come through no fault of your own, and it must be endured, not fought off as if it were unjust in its consequences. You can bear it with peace. To bear it bitterly and unwillingly only increases its weight. To think yourself undeserving during suffering is to resist the purpose of the trial. If you recognize the opportunity to submit to the will of God, the trial mercifully lightens as its purpose and profit are revealed to you.

Living a good life does not depend on continuous health and happiness but on understanding that what God has in store for you in time to come far exceeds any suffering you might endure today. Trials will remind you of your dependence on God. They are not designed to confound and discourage you, but to reveal your faith and will to you. God will make use of trials for your own good, to teach or show you something he knows will be to your ultimate benefit. We cannot see the extent of our future trials but be assured God supplies you with the strength and grace necessary to endure all trials. Even though your body or mind may waste away or be threatened with death, your spiritual strength will be constantly renewed if you depend on God and trust in what is unseen and yet to come.

You will also experience suffering simply because you are a believer in Christ. You will experience unpopularity, persecution, ridicule, sacrifice, and the toil of the Christian life. You could understandably think God's plan for you is always going to be a "good" plan, one with the intent of making your life overflow with joy and abundance. Yet, that is not true, for the Lord disciplines those he loves. Please understand his plans are not just to benefit you alone. He very likely intends to use you to teach or bless those around you.

God has a hopeful end in mind for you, if only you would wholeheartedly submit to him and wait patiently for it. In all conditions of life, it is our duty to live peaceful lives, patiently leaving it to God to work deliverance for us in due time. He will give us not the expectations of our fears but the expectations of our faith. What we receive, he has promised, will be what is best for us.

Always be prepared to give an answer when asked to explain the hope that you have during trials and suffering. Even if you should suffer for doing or saying what is right, you are blessed. If it is God's will, a harvest of righteousness and peace is your reward for not becoming weary of doing what is right. Evil will try to undo good works, but boldly facing evil strengthens what is good. Give in to your trials, and you begin to turn away from God. But remain faithful and pray to the Lord, and your appeals will be heard. You and your faith will be strengthened as a result of your trials and suffering. Remember, the Christian life has a certain blessedness that runs through it, ultimately concluding in your immeasurable joy. May you hold on to see this day! Amen.

Jesus said to him, "If you can believe,
all things are possible to him who believes."
Immediately the father of the child
cried out and said with tears,
"Lord, I believe; help my unbelief!"

MARK 9:23-24

Be anxious for nothing, but in everything
by prayer and supplication,
with thanksgiving, let your requests
be made known to God;
and the peace of God, which surpasses all understanding,
will guard your hearts and minds through Christ Jesus.

PHILIPPIANS 4:6-7

Worry and Doubt

BELOVED FRIEND, TAKE heart and do not worry. I know that is easier said than done, but worrisome thoughts distract you from that which you should dwell on, your Father in Heaven. So do your best to conquer your worry. There is much in life you cannot control, and there will be mysteries for which you may never find answers. So if you give in to worry, it will be your shadow, always following you. God cares for all of his creation from the birds in the sky, to the lilies of the field, to you. It is true that all things are not good, but God is working all things out for your good. Have faith that his plan for you is a good plan and believe that he does not want you to be made ineffective with worry and doubt.

Like worry, doubt is the handiwork of your enemy. Doubt about the truth of God will lead you to doubt that he was able to part the Red Sea, there once was a day longer than twenty-four hours because the sun did not set, Jonah survived in the belly of a whale, Jesus turned water into wine, and more than that, he rose from the dead. When you dismiss these and other miracles on the basis of their challenge to your powers of reason, you put aside the very evidence given to you that God is greater than anything you can comprehend. So, set aside worldly reason and just believe in God. Believe that God is God and, therefore, not limited to what you or I can understand. Praise him that he is grand on a scale far beyond our comprehension!

God gave you life, and he will see that it is nourished, if you would just trust in him. Turn away from worldly concerns, call on the Lord, and all things needed will be given to you. Do your duty with a full trust in God that he will see that you do not go without necessary things. Instead of worrying, lay your case before God, not as a complaint but with thanks for his mercy, and you will find the peace that comes after putting all in the hands of the one who is able and willing to help you prosper in righteousness.

Remember, worry and doubt are common struggles that stem from a lack of faith in God and his provision for you and can negatively affect your spiritual growth and relationship with him. Worry and doubt can be difficult to overcome, but by focusing on your faith in

God and bringing your worries and doubts to him in prayer, you will find peace in him. It is equally important to remember that God is in control and that he has had from the beginning of time a most thorough and appropriate plan for your life. Put your faith in and seek peace of mind in him. On that foundation, you can overcome your worry and doubt. There is no need for anxiety when you place your trust in God's good plan for you.

However, I urge you to be patient about this matter. God hears your prayers and pleas but answers in his own time. As with any trial, you must have patient endurance as you work through the strengthening of your confidence in God. Do not in impatient haste throw away your confidence but hold yourself up in unrelenting prayer. In time, when you have resisted doubt and believed God, you will be richly rewarded for your righteousness. May it always be so!

Jesus wept.

JOHN 11:35

But I do not want you to be ignorant, brethren,
concerning those who have fallen asleep,
lest you sorrow as others who have no hope.
For if we believe that Jesus died and rose again,
even so God will bring with Him those who sleep in Jesus.

1 THESSALONIANS 4:13-14

Loss and Grief

FRIEND, LIFE IS full of contrasts and juxtapositions. We will travel over mountains and go through valleys. We will enjoy pleasures and will suffer toils. We will have both victories and losses. One of the most challenging contrasts a man will wrestle with is this: how can a loving and compassionate God permit a loved one to die and break our hearts in such a devastating way? It is permissible to ask this question, and I have done so myself. I remember well my first heartbreak after losing to the grave someone dear to me. Grief is a powerful, even tormenting, emotion, one that Christ himself experienced at the loss of a friend. Yet, Jesus did not weep over the death itself because he knew his friend, Lazarus, would soon be raised from the dead, and ultimately, they would enjoy each other's company again in eternity in Heaven. The tears of Jesus were actually tears of joy.

We have this same hope for each other and all those we love who also believe in Christ. You must hold onto this truth to help you bear with your suffering in grief, and you must teach it to everyone, especially those you love so dearly. You now live in a broken world, one that is beneath Heaven and less in every way than our glorious future home. Unfortunately, our broken world includes all the painful consequences of sin, even death, and you must endure them for a time. Your sins deserve all manner of griefs and sorrows, even the most severe. You are saved from ruin, however, by the grace you have in Christ, who took your sins and just punishment upon himself. If you believe in him, you, too, have victory over death and will rise to live and love again. Joy in everlasting life is the great reward for the Christian. The joy you will have in all that awaits you in Heaven more than outweighs all the causes for your sorrows today.

I must warn you that my words here are easy to accept when you are not in the depths of sorrow, but it will be quite a different matter when your heart is broken with grief. You will be tempted to pray that God will not take your beloved child or companion. In that time, you must remember that making your requests with confidence does not mean that God will grant everything you might ask of him. If your request is not consistent with his will, when one of the most passionate and legitimate prayers of your life seems to go unanswered, you may feel abandoned and think God has let you down. Your faith may be shaken so badly that you doubt all the wonderful things I have been teaching you. This is an understandable reaction, and I assure you, a temporary one. Your pain will never be completely gone because you will always be aware of a beloved one's absence. But just as you might be filled with eager anticipation about the arrival of a cherished guest here on Earth, you can have that same anticipation about a reunion in Heaven. It may take your heart a bit to mend and begin to feel this anticipation, but it will come, and what a relief it will be for you.

Child of God, you will not be spared grief, but thanks be to Christ, neither will you be denied reunion. Believe this, and you will be uplifted by hope. May the unbelievers marvel at your composure as you suffer loss and grief and come to you begging to understand the reason for the hope that you have. Godspeed in that moment!

Now may the God of hope fill you with
all joy and peace in believing,
that you may abound in hope by the
power of the Holy Spirit.

ROMANS 15:13

My brethren, count it all joy when
you fall into various trials,
knowing that the testing of your faith produces patience.

JAMES 1:2-3

For it would have been better for them
not to have known the way of righteousness,
than having known it,
to turn from the holy commandment delivered to them.

2 PETER 2:21

Falling Away

THERE IS NO experience more painful than grief over the loss of a dearly loved one. That pain is so penetrating it cuts not only through the heart but into your faith, too. Sadly, grief will not be the only challenger of your faith. You will experience bitter disappointment or may suffer an unjust consequence or violence. You might even lose your health or abilities to injury or disease. When suffering like this after having given yourself to Jesus and trying so hard to walk the good walk, it would be understandable that you find it difficult to hold onto your faith.

There may be other reasons your faith is attacked, for the enemy is an insidious beast. You may think you are doing all the right things as a believer but do not see the promised blessings coming to you. You may pray passionately and often and think that God does not hear you or care to answer you. Perhaps there is no joy in your acts of service because no one seems to be grateful for your efforts. Maybe a friend demeans your faith and worship and belittles you in such a way that you wonder if Christian living is a worthy endeavor. At some point, one or more of these circumstances will become yours. Your spiritual strength will become weak, and you will wonder what to do or where to turn. You might even tell yourself you no longer believe.

Friend, we all have seasons of doubt, and when you are in that season, know that you are not alone. Many people begin to lose faith in God following cruel or unbearable life experiences. Feeling frustrated when your life takes an unexpected turn is understandable and okay. It is okay to be angry at God when you think he is not listening to you. But when you feel this distance from God, remember that he is not at all distant from you. His presence is constant, and he is closer to your situation than you may think. This is the time when you should call out to him. Bring to him your pain, frustration, and unmet expectations, knowing that he is a good Father and he cares about your concerns. He won't shame or condemn you. Be honest with him because he already knows what you think and feel. He is not angry with you for having doubts or struggling with unbelief; he understands your weaknesses and has compassion and empathy for you in these moments.

This may seem counterintuitive, but when you feel as though you are falling away from God, kneel and pray. Confess your unbelief and ask that it be restored. Continue to worship him. God wants you to reach out to him in faith, even when your faith seems to be slipping away. He wants you to trust him even when it seems there is very little reason to do so. Summon up the resolve to continue your relationship with God. He will not refuse you but will welcome you back, for he promised that all who seek him will indeed find him.

My friend, do not keep your failing faith a secret and attempt to restore it by yourself. God wants you in fellowship with other Christians so that you can be helped when you are burdened. The more you hide and pretend, the worse the challenge will become. I am, as are your other friends in Christ, ready to pray with you and encourage you through the time. Share your doubts with someone strong in the faith who would have the wisdom and discernment, as well as the compassion, to guide you back to belief. Not only will you experience the blessing of working out your faith with someone who desires your success in that endeavor, but you might also be surprised and helped at the same time to learn that even the most passionate evangelists have experienced falling away from God.

I pray that you never begin to fall away, but should

you, let a brother or sister help you, my friend. You will be reminded that grace is unmerited, and Christ's love is unconditional; and because of that, you have not, nor cannot lose your salvation. May knowing that people are interceding on your behalf give you the determination to be restored to the initial joy you had when you were sure of God and trusted his ways. May the Holy Spirit bring you peace and solace and fill your thoughts with the goodness of God. And may all the angels sing when the lost sheep is found! Amen.

Let us not become conceited,
provoking one another, envying one another.

GALATIANS 5:26

Let your conduct be without covetousness;
be content with such things as you have.
For He Himself has said, "I will never
leave you nor forsake you."

HEBREWS 13:5

Envy

FRIEND, DO NOT fall in with the customs of those who walk in the lusts of the flesh and give the best share of their attention and effort to earthly things. You have a treasure that will never rust or decay, a treasure stored up for you in Heaven, one that lasts in eternity. What treasure is better than what you already have? The children of God live not to please the cravings of the flesh but according to the incorrupt nature of the Spirit. Therefore, worldly treasures should not captivate and rule over you. Neither should any of the blessings that others may enjoy, be they beauty, creativity, influence, or acclaim, result in your envy. Those blessings may seem attractive or valuable, but they are fleeting because they are of the world and cannot last forever.

To envy or covet is to not be content with what the Lord has given you. To envy is to indulge a desire for more, to have a longing for worldly things, accompanied by dissatisfaction with your present circumstances. You will discover envy within yourself if you realize you prefer worldly excess to righteous moderation. If you keep all your earnings for your own profit instead of making generous or sacrificial offerings for the benefit of others, you are motivated by envy. If you spend all your time and talent seeking the praise and rewards of men rather than pursuing the glory of God and the interests of the church, you are motivated by envy. When you covet, you assign a higher priority to your own interests and pleasures than to God. When your own satisfaction becomes your primary goal, you have taken on an idol, and it is you.

Envy is a destructive emotion that can lead you away from God and your purpose in life. It relentlessly increases the feeling of not being content with what you have been given. Be cautious, because envy often comes from a desire for things that you do not truly need. As a Christian, you are called to practice gratitude and contentment in all circumstances. Your Christian duties cannot be performed out of unselfish love and unambitious intentions when you suffer with envy. Envy can be a difficult emotion to overcome, but by focusing on gratitude and thanking God for his present blessings, you can resist the urge to envy.

Dear friend, be content with present things, with

present riches or present poverty, with present benefits or burdens, with present affirmations or reproaches. Your contentment with these things shows itself in your thankfulness for every tender mercy, and by your eager submission to the will of God in every state and circumstance of your life.

I remind you, we have treasures in Heaven that cannot be measured; it is promised to us and awaits you now. Knowing what lies ahead, an immeasurable treasure that cannot be taken from you by any man, you can and should be content with what you now have in this temporary world. But more than that, you have the gracious presence of God with you, now in life, later at death, and then forever after in Heaven. What can be better? Amen!

Do not judge, and you will not be judged.
Do not condemn, and you will not be condemned.
Forgive, and you will be forgiven.

LUKE 6:37

Judgment

CHILD OF GOD, do not judge others. It is a tempting thing to find fault and error in others, but judgment does not build others up. It is easy to assume that you know better or have all the answers, or worse, that you may be a better person than another. Such thoughts are not beneficial. You must remember that you yourself are not perfect, so take care not to offend others with harsh judgment lest you be judged as well.

Rather than judge, be gentle with others, lifting them up with your kind words and deeds. Do this, and you will be blessed with many friends. It is said a house divided against itself cannot stand; neither can the body of believers. Put aside differences and unite as believers, strengthening each other and the church for the sake of Christ. Avoid rash judgments and a desire to find fault in others. God respects moral character, not appearances, wealth, or earthly rank. Put aside all temptation to judge others and rid yourself of this unrighteous behavior. And guard your mind, or it will wander in the direction of thinking more highly of yourself than others.

As a Christian, you are called to love and accept all people, regardless of their actions or beliefs. Instead of judging, strive to show everyone compassion and understanding. In everything you do, help those who are weak in strength, self-control, and faith. Bear with their shortcomings; do not exploit them. And remember Jesus' compassion for those unable to help themselves except by their dependence on him. Do this always, not just when it serves you well. To judge is not only unjust but also decidedly unfair. Look to the interests of all others and earn respect for your impartial, equitable character rather than contempt for your unfair and biased ways. Your lack of judgment will be seen as an increase in your grace.

I know you want to ask me if it is realistic to never judge anyone. Let me remind you that God gave you the power of discernment, and Christ said to be sly while living in the broken world. There are times when judgment is necessary, but only when necessary to reach an honest evaluation about a person or situation so that you might do or say the right thing, and never to belittle someone else so that you might puff yourself up.

Jesus asked you to stop searching for the shortcomings of others and to look inwardly to examine your heart and motives. He knew that if you focus on your own faults and weaknesses instead of those of someone else, you would become more empathetic with your neighbors, perhaps even your enemies.

Do not forget that justice belongs only to the sovereign Lord. Rid yourself of a wrathful mind. If it is possible, as far as you have any say or influence in the matter, live at peace with everyone. Do not forget that your own actions and thoughts will be judged just as harshly as those you may judge. By refraining from judgment, you will show love and forgiveness to all, just as God shows love and forgiveness to you.

Finally, while it is right to hate sin, it is not right to hate the sinner. It is God's job to deal with the sinner, and your job to love and accept all, even those who may not believe or act as you think they should. Again, refrain from judgment, offer grace, and you will become an example for others to follow. May you always be known for your unbiased and benevolent behavior, and your increasing effort to think generously of others. Amen.

A fool has no delight in understanding,
but in expressing his own heart.

PROVERBS 18:2

He who answers a matter before he hears it,
it is folly and shame to him.

PROVERBS 18:13

Whoever guards his mouth and tongue
keeps his soul from troubles.

PROVERBS 21:23

Listening

MY FRIEND, BE quick to listen, slow to speak, and slow to anger. It sounds simple enough, but it is a way of relating to others that is nearly impossible to master. It is so difficult because you have a natural tendency to want to be right in all things, and listening seems counterproductive when you already have the answers that satisfy you. Consequently, in your youth, you will surely be slow to listen, quick to speak, and quick to anger. Such behavior will only push people away from you, and I doubt that is what you want. I urge you to remember these sayings: Poor listening rejects, but good listening understands, and poor listening diminishes, but good listening lifts up. Thankfully, if it is your goal, you will get better at listening with time.

Good listening requires discipline, concentration, patience, and intentionality, qualities that will come to you slowly but surely if you seek them. I urge you to become a patient and attentive listener. Listening is an important aspect of the Christian walk. You cannot attend to others if you do not hear their needs. It is not just about hearing the words that are spoken to you, but truly listening with an open heart and mind. You should be more interested in listening to others with the goal of understanding than in planning your response. Listening is not about making yourself heard; rather, it is about gaining a profound understanding. When listening with an open heart and mind, you can deepen your relationships with others and gain a better understanding of their needs, hurts, and perspectives — insight you should have if you are to be helpful. Remember, you cannot share good news with anyone who avoids you if you are known to dominate conversations or listen carelessly.

Listening is also an essential component of your relationship with God. By taking the time to listen to God in prayer and meditation, you will gain a deeper understanding of his will and guidance for your life. It is a discipline that requires much practice, but once developed it can bring great benefits to your daily interactions and your spiritual growth. Will God speak directly to you? I do not know. But I strongly believe he speaks to us through his Word. If the Bible is God-breathed, and I believe that it is, then it may as well be him speaking to you as you read it.

The purpose of the Scriptures is to inspire hope in you through the promises and comfort they offer to those who live for God. Everything that was written was written to teach you so that through the encouragement of the Scriptures, you might become fully equipped, able to teach the Gospel to others and to discourage its opposers. When reading your Bible, listen to what it says!

I pray that you listen well, both to God and man, and glorify God in all other things that you hear and answer to. Amen.

And walk in love, as Christ also has
loved us and given Himself for us,
speaking to one another in psalms and
hymns and spiritual songs,
singing and making melody in your heart to the Lord,
giving thanks always for all things to God the Father
in the name of our Lord Jesus Christ,
submitting to one another in the fear of God.

EPHESIANS 5:2, 19-20

Friendship and Fellowship

FRIENDSHIP IS A gift from God and an important opportunity for sharing the experience of Christian living. Friendship is a way to connect with others, to support each other, to learn from each other, and to grow together in faith. Friends are a reminder that you are not alone in your journey and that through friendship, you will enjoy love, support, and encouragement. True friends are there for one another in good times and bad, offering comfort and help. Make many of these kinds of friends by being one yourself for others.

Making friends begins with remembering that Jesus said, "Love your neighbor." Wake up every day and ask yourself, "What can I do for my family and friends today?" If, instead, your thoughts are about you, your goals, your dreams, and your ambitions, you are inwardly focused, thinking selfishly rather than selflessly. Yes, I know, it is such a challenge to be selfless, but it is a worthy goal, nonetheless. Encourage your friends and stir them to do good deeds so that your fellowship in Jesus might increase. It is through relationships with others that you will grow in your faith and support others as they navigate their own unique journey. Christ, the perfect one without sin, laid down his life for us, sinners, and in return asked that we give comfort to those in trouble, sharing the comfort that we first received from him. If you love as he loved, you cannot refuse to comfort your suffering brother. Let your love for others be deep and enduring, not shallow and brief, and you will be a good friend indeed.

Remember, to be a good friend may mean speaking an unwelcome truth. Do not hesitate to speak boldly but kindly to your friends and turn them away from false hope and worldly concerns. Do this carefully, with concern and compassion, never with self-righteous scolding. Do this bravely, not fearfully, for speaking up at all on heavenly matters is a confession of how much you care. If you care about them in this life, how much more you should care about them in the next! Be zealous, enthusiastic, and accepting, making the needs of your friends your own and helping them, caring for one another in the same loving fellowship as Christ cares for you. Make yourself welcome with your encouraging and uplifting words. Encourage your friends and stir them to do good deeds so that the cause of Christ may be made stronger in number. You will be richly rewarded when you grow together in Jesus.

It is important to seek and nurture friendships, especially those that help you grow in your faith. On the other hand, bad company corrupts good character, period. Unfortunately, everyone will not want to be your friend. Do not be led astray by the unbelievers who may mock your faith. Turn to the body of believers for your spiritual companionship and fortification, and bask in the fellowship of that safe refuge, for the church and its members are a safe harbor from the pains of darkness. It is better to have a few righteous friends than many friends who would lead you down a path of corruption and deceit.

Beloved, do not let yourself be upset by what others might say about you. Let them talk. People, especially those who do not share in our faith, are so often vain, hurtful, arrogant, and hypocritical. The world will always be the world, so let the water flow beneath the bridge. All you need to be concerned with is seeking the will of God. Remember, you can't please everyone, and it isn't worth the effort. But you can please the Lord. He is your best friend. One moment of his pleasure will heal any wound inflected on you by mere people. Your detractors will come and go, but God is always with you. Amen!

The wicked is ensnared by the transgression of his lips,
but the righteous will come through trouble.

PROVERBS 12:13

Better is a little with righteousness,
than vast revenues without justice.

PROVERBS 16:8

But above all, my brethren, do not swear,
either by heaven or by earth or with any other oath.
But let your "Yes" be "Yes,"
and your "No," "No," lest you fall into judgment.

JAMES 5:12

Honesty

HONESTY IS A necessary component of relationships because it is the foundation of trust. Mutual trust is essential for any relationship to grow, thrive, and remain healthy. When individuals are honest with each other, they establish mutual trust that they can rely on and believe each other in all situations.

Therefore, my dear friend, simply let your Yes be Yes, and your No be No. Be aware of how simple it is for the tongue to commit a wrong! You are a member of the Christian household, and every member deserves the truth. Do not lie, not even a little. Have faith and trust the results of honoring and defending the truth, the whole truth, especially the truth that salvation is found only through a wholehearted belief in Jesus Christ. If you have uttered any dishonesty, confess it, then turn away from that wrongful practice and conduct your-self as a new and better person, one who values and practices honesty in all your dealings. You glorify God when your honesty uplifts and encourages others, and you dishonor him when you spread falsehoods designed to misrepresent and lead others astray.

I remind you that the tongue can be a soothing comfort or a deadly weapon. Words are either lasting solace or lethal poison, depending on your control of your tongue. Your words should always reflect the good things stored up in you and be pleasing to the Lord. Do not utter both blessing and cursing, good and evil, about those you know and encounter. Such contradictions only insult God, for he made all people, and contradictions discourage your listeners. Your job is one of being an encouragement to others, so think before speaking and use carefully measured yet truthful words.

The challenge with honesty is that sometimes telling the truth can be uncomfortable to both you and your listener. Be not deterred by such discomfort. Rather, pray that God be with you, helping you to choose kind words. You may become tempted to condemn someone you believe to be preoccupied with evil. Be cautious in these times. You may well be right in your assessment of evil, but will your condemnation, even though truthful, result in an opportunity to help another better their circumstances? Will it help you to share the good news of the Gospel? Your Christian walk will always be in the midst of evil and brokenness, yet you are to occupy yourself with all that is good and peaceful. Do this, and the love and grace of God will pervade your heart and be revealed in the words you speak. Do this, and your words will achieve mutual understanding instead of mutual resentment.

You can be your authentic Christian self in all relationships while you practice honesty with a gentle tongue. May the God of peace be with you always, finding pleasure in your honest and careful words. Amen.

Rejoice with those who rejoice, and
weep with those who weep.
Be of the same mind toward one another.

ROMANS 12:15-16

Therefore let us pursue the things which make for peace
and the things by which one may edify another.

ROMANS 14:19

Be at peace among yourselves.

1 THESSALONIANS 5:13

Peace and Harmony

WHEN LIVING IN harmony with one another, we share the love of Christ and become examples of the goodness that is accomplished in his name. But if living in conflict with one another, we work against his purpose and distract everyone from the message of reconciliation as told in the Gospel. You are called to not just live in peace and harmony in as much as you can control yourself with those nearest you, but you are a messenger, an ambassador, and a peacemaker meant to spread goodwill among all people so that everyone might live together in peace and harmony. I pray that you excel in this endeavor!

Friend, live and encourage a peaceful life. Christ understood that for the Gospel to be made known, believers must be peace-loving rather than quarrelsome so that those who have not yet heard the Word would listen rather than turn away. Don't participate in or encourage foolish and stupid arguments, because you know they lead to conflict rather than peace. Opposers of the Word must be corrected, but not rudely; rather, gently, kindly, and humbly. Jesus drew people to himself, and in his gentle company, they stopped and listened to his message. Be like-minded, be a purveyor of peace and harmony, and make yourself welcome and heard.

Though it may seem not your place, be willing to step into discord and conflict, especially within your own circle of family, friends, and neighbors, and from a position of neutrality, seek to resolve matters and restore peace and harmony so that division does not get a foothold. Let peace thwart the work of the enemy!

Keep in mind that you yourself are not infallible and without fault, so judge others' circumstances gently. Show no sign of favoritism, deceit, or exploitation, for such conduct only divides and destroys. Child of God, take a spirit of harmony wherever you go. If you are filled with the love of Christ, peace will reign in your heart and be evident in your words and deeds. There must not be disagreement, separation, or rebellion between you and others, for without peace no one will see and understand the healing reconciliation of the Lord. Let your conduct be thoughtful and wise, and you will stir many neighbors to live in the same way. Do not provoke criticism, annoyance, or rejection, yet say what is honest and best for every occasion and always in a spirit of love sprinkled with grace.

Beloved, you and yours, strive daily to live in harmony with one another. Be sympathetic, love each other as family, and be compassionate and humble. Do not repay evil with evil or insult with insult, but with blessing, because to bless is why you were called into the service of the Lord. Who is going to harm you if you are eager to do good?

I pray that you always be prepared to answer anyone who asks you to explain the reason for the hope and peace that you have – that you are reconciled to God through Jesus Christ – and that conversation gives glory to God. Amen!

Remember this: Whoever sows sparingly
will also reap sparingly,
and whoever sows generously will also reap generously.
Each of you should give what you have
decided in your heart to give,
not reluctantly or under compulsion,
for God loves a cheerful giver.

2 CORINTHIANS 9:6-8

By this we know love, because He
laid down His life for us.
And we also ought to lay down our lives for the brethren.
But whoever has this world's goods,
and sees his brother in need,
and shuts up his heart from him,
how does the love of God abide in him?

1 JOHN 3:16-17

Generosity and Sacrifice

CHILD OF GOD, the Lord gave himself for you, what shall you give for him? All that you have is not your own but was provided to you by God. He created everything; nothing is the handiwork of man outside the influence of God. Yes, he even invented money. And money, as well as anything else you have, is provided to you not only to assure your comfort and entertainment but also to prosper you so that you may be a help to others. Make the needs of others your own and help them, giving freely and cheerfully. Share what he has given you, and, in the process, please and honor him who has made you rich in Heaven.

Jesus told us to use our earthly resources to gain friends by making a real difference in their lives, and then lead them to him. Therefore, do not hold on tightly to what you have been blessed with, but share it for the greater good. The resources that God has entrusted to you should be used honorably and in a manner that is glorifying to him. To share is more than being nice; it is a form of thanksgiving and praise. Make the needs of others your concern and share as needed to provide relief from an immediate crisis. Let me emphasize *share as needed*, which may be more than you think you can let go of. Friend, letting go is the very point. Do not hoard for yourself for that brings no glory to God. Give, and then give some more. Such sacrifices please the Lord and bring glory to his name. Share more than just your treasure and possessions, but your heart, counsel, talent, and time, too. Your free and cheerful sharing of God's gifts to you will indeed be a blessing to others, and to you as well.

Be careful to avoid using charity to heap praise upon yourself or to manipulate others for your devious uses. Generosity without God in it may be your way of seeking praise, to prove to yourself and others what a good person you are, or to gain an advantage. If these are your motives, your reward will be fleeting. Greed and ambition are worldly strivings that will only bring discontent to your heart. Your inner peace will be destroyed by a heart of discontent if you are spurred on in the pursuit of your own glory.

Every day, you will be tempted to think of and take care of yourself first. Does your mind busy itself with obsessions about how others may benefit you? Are you willing to sacrifice someone for your gain, or yourself for the sake of someone else? When you are faced with these questions, ask yourself, "Who is able to fill you with significance, man, or God?" Why would you be willing to be poured out and left with less in the evening than you had in the morning? Because it pleases the Lord. Why does it please the Lord? Your willing sacrifice of any of your resources shows that you have freed yourself of selfish motives and chosen to live a life aiming only to please God. When you are motivated only by your love of God, no sacrifice is too great, and no humiliation too painful. Sacrifice for the benefit of others out of reverence for Christ and give freely and unselfishly as he gave himself freely and unselfishly for you.

Friend, set aside today any thoughts of worldly rewards and remember that whoever sows sparingly will also reap sparingly, and whoever sows generously will also reap generously. Do not hesitate to give yourself away, for with such sacrifices God is well pleased. May he always be well pleased with you! Amen.

Be kindly affectionate to one another with brotherly love,
in honor giving preference to one another;
not lagging in diligence, fervent in
spirit, serving the Lord;
rejoicing in hope, patient in tribulation,
continuing steadfastly in prayer;
distributing to the needs of the saints, given to hospitality.

ROMANS 12:10-13

Service

FRIEND, CHRIST DEMONSTRATED his love by
serving others. Everywhere he went, he took care of the
immediate needs of all whom he encountered. He did
not first require their acknowledgment of his deity or
expect something in return for his deeds. He simply took
care of people as he saw the need to do so. You should
do likewise. Do good deeds simply because good deeds
need to be done, not to gain recognition from men or
rewards in Heaven. It is the deed motivated by grace
and humility that shines and pleases God. Be careful
not to do righteous and generous things only because
you seek applause and praise. Take an honest look at
your motives and choose to humble yourself before
others, for God lifts up the humble servant. Remember
that it is one thing to serve others motivated only by
the goal of being a good person, and quite another to
serve because you are moved by deep Christian love.

The latter is much more noble than the former. The call to all Christians is to do good deeds, with those deeds wrapped in love, not for any personal gain whatsoever, including self-satisfaction (even praising yourself in your private thoughts is to seek your own glory). Recall your purpose and do good deeds to bring glory to God.

Let me point out that there are many burdens: financial, spiritual, emotional, and physical. To the extent you are able, help lighten others' burdens, whatever they may be. Serve not because you must but because you are willing and eager to be of help to your fellow man, your neighbor, in honor of Christ. Again, Christ demonstrated his love by serving others, and he offered his life to save yours. Therefore, with a heart grateful for your salvation, care for others, serving them as often as you can, all the while urging them on to their own good deeds. When you are serving others, not only can you put your faith into action and help others see the ways in which God is working in the world, you will find opportunities to explain why you do what you may be doing. Blessed be the day that you explain to someone that it is not your goodness, but Christ alive in you — that is the reason for your service.

I should remind you that you, just as I am, even though saved in Christ and committed to Christian ideals, are a broken person as long as you are alive in this world. That means that you will continue to wrestle with things that are not holy, including anger and resentment when someone appears ungrateful for what you have done for them. Be careful here, for that reaction is fueled by selfish judgment that all too quickly may lead to wrath. It is best to be merciful in your thoughts. Perhaps your beneficiary does not know how to express gratitude or is slow to trust your motive. Be patient and forgiving, and continue on in willing service knowing that God in Heaven is pleased with you. Remember always that he is who you serve, and your deeds are never unnoticed. May all the angels rejoice as they witness your acts of service! May the Lord be pleased to greet you with these words, "Well done, good and faithful servant!" Amen.

Wait on the Lord;
be of good courage,
and He shall strengthen your heart;
wait, I say, on the Lord!

PSALM 27:14

My brethren, count it all joy when
you fall into various trials,
knowing that the testing of your faith produces patience.
But let patience have its perfect work,
that you may be perfect and complete, lacking nothing.

JAMES 1:2-4

Patience

FRIEND, THE LORD is full of compassion and mercy but works in his own time. Resist impatience, stand firm in your conviction, and remain confident as you wait. The faith that endures earns the crown. Remember God's promise: he will not burden you with more than you can bear. Under God's plan, all things, even your sorrow, trials, and persecutions, work together for your blessing.

Do nothing that would discourage others from turning to Christ, but instead, let the Holy Spirit use you to inspire others to follow Christ. If your heart is filled with love, patience will be one of your defining qualities and the reason why others draw nearer to you. Your abundant patience with others leaves time for anger and impulse to fade away. Pray that your patience will increase, for you will certainly need much more than you might think.

Patience is a virtue that is often easier described than lived out, but it is a virtue that is so necessary for your spiritual growth. Patience allows you to wait on the Lord and to place your trust in him. In this fast-paced world, it can be difficult to slow down and wait for things to unfold in their own time. But as a Christian, you are called to have patience and trust in God's timing and plan for your life. It is important to remember that God's timing is not your own. You must be patient and trust that he will bring about the best result in his perfect timing. In praying for increased patience and faith, your relationship with God will deepen, and you will find peace in knowing that he is in control of all your circumstances.

Patience will help you to control your emotions and reactions, rather than leaving you to act impulsively. Patience allows you to take a step back and consider a challenging situation from a broader perspective, rather than getting caught up in the narrow focus of an emotional moment. Patience can help you to understand and empathize with others, rather than to judge or criticize them quickly and harshly. Patience helps you to persevere and bounce back from difficult situations, rather than giving up easily. Patience will help you to trust in God's plan and timing, rather than trying to control everything with your own means and plans. Have patience, and you will have peace. Have I convinced you yet of the importance of patience?

Remarkably, when your faith is tested, your patience has an opportunity to grow. Friend, this means that patience and faith go hand-in-hand. Through trials and difficulties, your patience and faith will be tested, but if you trust in God and have patience, you will become stronger in your faith. Be faithful and patient and submit to his timing, and he will not forget you nor lead you astray. Amen.

Let him who stole steal no longer,
but rather let him labor,
working with his hands what is good,
that he may have something to give him who has need.

EPHESIANS 4:28

And whatever you do, do it heartily,
as to the Lord and not to men,
knowing that from the Lord you will receive
the reward of the inheritance; for
you serve the Lord Christ.

COLOSSIANS 3:23-24

Work

EVERYONE IS TO work so that he might provide for himself and not be a burden to others, but also, and perhaps more importantly, to be able to help others in their time of need. In all that you do, you are a representative of Christ; therefore, in whatever work you apply yourself, do it with all your heart as though you are working for the Lord. To this end, spare no time, self-denial, or effort, for it pleases the Lord when you do your work well. Work is not only an opportunity to serve God and others, but it also allows you to fulfill your purpose on Earth. By using your talents and abilities to work, you fulfill the purpose that God created you for. Your work is a way to serve and make a positive impact in the world for the increase of glory to God.

Do as much as you can in line with your blessings and abilities, no matter how high or low the task may be, with joy in your heart, knowing you are a model of Christ's great love and mercy. You cannot do everything, but you can do something. Do something and do it well, even if the task seems small. The good deeds demonstrated in the course of your work may well be a pivotal moment of inspiration to someone else.

Friend, you are also called to be a responsible steward of the gifts and talents that God has given you. This includes using your abilities and resources to work for the betterment of yourself, your family, and your community. Through your commitment to work, you have the opportunity to serve and glorify God. You are blessed with gifts as you are best able to use them, just as others are blessed with different gifts for different uses. God's gifts to us vary in manner and form, but all should be committed to the service of the Lord. Use your gifts in your work, and you will find delight in your labor. This pleases the Lord.

Consider this — to occupy yourself in honest labor is the best remedy for a dishonest life. I do not think you are dishonest, but I do think the avoidance of work leads to scheming thoughts and worse, manipulation of others for selfish benefit. Both are harmful to your growth as a Christian. Instead, work hard so that you might become better able to help others. To do something for someone in need is pleasing to Christ. When you do for others, your good deeds motivated by faith will be witnessed by many. This, too, pleases the Lord. Lend your helping hands as often as you are able, doing whatever is needed. If you render good service anywhere to anyone, the Lord will see that you are rewarded.

Friend, there is no doubt that, at times, work may seem fruitless and exhausting. I tell you, that may be the time that you should lean into it more. Work teaches discipline, responsibility, and perseverance. These are important qualities for leading an exemplary Christian life. Laziness is not a virtue, and neither is taking advantage of others so that you might work less. I encourage you to work and work hard. I pray you find joy in your toil, so much joy that your work hardly seems like toil at all. May it be so!

There remains therefore a rest for the people of God.
For he who has entered His rest has himself
also ceased from his works as God did from His.

HEBREWS 4:9-10

Rest

ALONG WITH LIVING in simplicity, you must make time to rest. I do not mean naps or brief periods of mindless pause. I mean intentionally planning for and setting aside time to number your blessings, to study and meditate on the teachings of Christ, and to give thanks for your salvation. Jesus does want you to work but does not want you to be forever weary and burdened; he wants you to enjoy rest. He gave himself as an example for finding rest not only for your body, but also your soul. Even God rested from his glorious works of creation. God gives the weekly Sabbath to remind you of his never-ending faithful provision. Honor the Sabbath and rest.

Believe me, to truly hear and understand God's voice, you need to be still and quiet your mind. True rest is a source of refreshment, a time for rejuvenation, and a means to a better relationship with God and other people. Rest affords you the time to recognize current difficulties as momentary afflictions compared to the eternal rest that awaits you in Heaven. Rest is an opportunity to reflect on God's goodness and deepen your relationship with him. To rest restoratively is to focus your mind on Jesus and the perfect, painless, and joyful future that awaits all who follow him.

Friend, it can be particularly difficult to rest when the circumstances of life lead to conflict with others, fears of all the things that could go wrong, or anxiety about what others may expect of you. God desires rest for you because deep, relaxing rest in the face of these difficulties will not come naturally to you. To rest, you must trust that he will take care of critical things for you. You must trust that if you take a day off, the world will not break down and spin into chaos. To experience deep rest, you must be attentive and intentional about what thoughts fill your mind. You should think about things that are good and true and beautiful, and imagine the glorious future that awaits all those who rest in Christ.

If you lack rest, you will suffer physically, mentally, emotionally, and spiritually. Physical and mental exhaustion often lead to emotional turmoil, including anger, bitterness, and impatience. The lack of rest will certainly cause tension in your most important relationships, including your relationship with God. You must establish a rhythm of work and rest to live up to your potential. Work gives you the opportunity to partner with God in his goals for creation, while rest lets you enter communion with God in the enjoyment of his creation. Too much work and all becomes drudgery. Not enough rest, and you will not be as thankful as you should be.

A last word — rest is essential for your spiritual well-being. It allows you to have a clear mind, to renew your heart and spirit, and to boldly face the challenges of your coming days and weeks. May you rest often in the deep well of peace and assurance that God is all that you need. Amen.

For the Lord loves the just and will
not forsake his faithful ones.

Psalm 37:28

You shall love the Lord your God with all your heart
and with all your soul and with all your mind.

Matthew 22:37

But without faith it is impossible to please Him,
for he who comes to God must believe that He is,
and that He is a rewarder of those
who diligently seek Him.

Hebrews 11:6

Faithfulness and Fidelity

FRIEND, THIS LETTER is of great importance. I must warn you that in the matter of faith, divided loyalties of any kind will lead you astray. Turn quickly from the temptation to cherry-pick attractive morsels from the various religions and philosophies of the world and instead submit yourself wholly and willfully only to God. You are to rid yourself of your former ways of life and put on a new self, one created to be like God in righteousness and holiness devoted to the only truth, his Word. Do not complicate your life with unholy philosophies and alliances; rather, commit yourself exclusively to the one and only true God. Anything less than this is most unfaithful and counterproductive for the Christian. You should be willing and able to defend your religion in the righteous fear of God. Never give in to the urge to cast God aside in favor of worldly allures and popular but unholy convictions. Let there be no room for other fears, especially rejection, to result in your disloyalty to God, your Creator.

This faithfulness, I mean to impress upon you, is a hallmark of the Christian life. It is the quality of being loyal, devoted, and committed to God, his teachings only, and his purpose only for the entirety of your life. Faithfulness is not only about being loyal to God but also being loyal to your commitments, whether they are to your family, friends, or community. Faithfulness is the forerunner of trust; thus, it is an important ingredient in our relationship with God. It confirms that you believe in him alone, that you rely on him alone, and that you are confident enough with his promises that you have no need for a safety net.

The evidence that you have a saving knowledge of Christ is loyal obedience to his commandments, including loving God with all your heart, soul, strength, and mind. You see, there is no part of you to be left for anything else. Although saved, we remain imperfect people who continue to be tempted by our sinful nature. Do not take salvation for granted and act as though you are unchanged. Train yourself to be godly, obey the Word, and rise above your nature, demonstrating your renewal so that others may wish to follow your example of faithfulness. Your singular loyalty to God is the sign of your sheer delight and joyful thankfulness for your salvation.

Let me remind you now that a Christian marriage is a relationship of mutual obligations entered into in the presence of God. Each spouse must offer to the other what is necessary to honor the vows entered into before God. Indeed, one of the most evident ways a Christian displays faithfulness is in the care and attention given to nurturing and protecting the marriage. Your spouse is a great blessing given to you so that you may more fully enjoy your life. Honor and treasure that blessing. You are called to love your spouse just as Christ loved the church, with loving devotion and lifelong fidelity. Love and give yourself to your spouse in absolute faithfulness, as it pleases the Lord.

Finally, my friend, rejoice in the Lord and celebrate the power of the Gospel to comfort one who has turned to Christ. Thanks be to God for the victory over sin and death through Christ! Amen.

Ascribe to the Lord the glory due his name;
worship the Lord in the splendor of holiness.

Psalm 29:2

Therefore let us be grateful for receiving
a kingdom that cannot be shaken,
and thus let us offer to God acceptable worship,
with reverence and awe.

Hebrews 12:28

Worship and Discipleship

GOD IS MAJESTIC, omniscient, omnipresent, and omnipotent. He is all-knowing. He is present everywhere. He is powerful in every way. He is worthy of glory and honor and praise. This is the reason for worship, to give the Father his due. Beloved friend, I encourage you to keep company with fellow believers, especially in the church. Christian worship is a community where believers share in the common experience of praising God and expressing their love, gratitude, and devotion to him. You were not created to be alone; you are meant to live in community. Worship is a holy activity, and the church is the place where you will experience blessings not to be found elsewhere, for there are some graces and blessings that God gives only in the meeting together with other believers. Worshipping God means you are ascribing worthiness to God for who he is and for what he has done for you. Make worship a priority in your life. Worship also serves as a reminder of God's love, grace, and power, and it helps to strengthen your faith and deepen your relationship with him. Through worship, you will experience encouragement and support from others, and you will be reminded that you are not alone in your faith journey.

Worship takes many forms, including singing, prayer, reading Scripture, preaching, and participating in the sacraments. It is an act of humility and surrender as you acknowledge your dependence on God and your gratitude for all he has done for you. Thus, worship helps realign your focus on God and his purposes and puts your worries, doubts, and fears into perspective. It will also help you prepare for another responsibility: to disciple those new to or weak in the faith.

Your spiritual health and well-being will eventually motivate you to the worthy work of making disciples. Discipleship involves serving and reaching out to others as a representative of Christ. As you grow in your faith, you are called to share it with others to help them grow in their faith as well. Simply put, you are to put your faith into action and be an example of Jesus to the world. This is accomplished through the joint study of the Bible and offering guidance as a spiritual mentor. As you mentor others in the faith, helping to interpret and apply the teachings of Jesus in your lives and circumstances, you become more like Jesus in your thoughts, words, and actions, and better able to reflect his love and grace to everyone. If you establish a regular practice of discipleship, you will help raise up the next generation of believers to follow Jesus earnestly.

New Christians often know little about the faith they profess to believe. Your challenge is teaching and training them and investing your heartfelt best interest in them. Your concern for them will help deepen and grow their faith in Christ as the newer believer follows your example of a seasoned Christian who has already walked through many of life's everyday challenges. Through discipleship, you will introduce accountability into the new believer's life, beginning with the basics and urging them toward a deeper understanding of Christian theology. This is a lot of responsibility, but you are up to it. And the Holy Spirit will help you. Fear not!

Friend, as more believers understand and live out Jesus' teachings, our churches will become more vital and faithful to our Lord. Worship and discipleship should be ongoing activities throughout your life. I pray that you will delight in them always. May it be so!

Go therefore and make disciples of all the nations,
baptizing them in the name of the Father
and of the Son and of the Holy Spirit,
teaching them to observe all things
that I have commanded you;
and lo, I am with you always, even to the end of the age.

MATTHEW 28:19-20

The word is near you, in your mouth and in your heart
(that is, the word of faith which we preach):
that if you confess with your mouth the Lord Jesus
and believe in your heart that God
has raised Him from the dead,
you will be saved.

ROMANS 10:8-9

Evangelism

BELOVED, ON THESE matters, I have much to tell you. It is written, "I believed; therefore, I have spoken," (Psalm 116:10, 2 Corinthians 4:13). Let these words remind you that your faith is not only to be enjoyed silently in your daily thoughts but is to be shared with others in publicly spoken words. God's plan for man's salvation and reconciliation to himself was never meant to be a secret. Jesus preached to thousands in the name of the Father, warning, teaching, and healing them. He instructed his disciples to go out and make disciples of all nations, and they, in turn, instructed us to share and teach the Scriptures. This instruction is given to you as well. At some point in your life, you will encounter an opportunity to tell someone about the Christian faith, and you must be prepared to do so in a way they can understand and accept as truth. The Holy Spirit will work within you as you share the good news; therefore, have faith, speak publicly, and good words will come forth from your mouth. Faith in the Gospel, nourished in the heart and openly confessed, will secure your salvation. Your belief must be more than a mental exercise; it should bring all your fiber into a loving trust and willing obedience to Christ. As often as you can, share the good news of the Gospel.

All around us are people who have never heard that God loves them and desires an abundant life for them. Most people you know do their best to live decent lives while searching for meaning and purpose. When they see that you have found meaning and purpose in Jesus, they will likely want to know how they can have the same joy you have. They need to hear the good news. The Lord asks you to tell others about him so that you can spread his message to the world. At all times, conduct yourself as though you belong to the Lord, and when asked why you behave as you do, eagerly explain his influence in your life. Use encouraging, motivating words; let Christ be honored and praised in your answer, claiming him as the reason for your hope. Don't be embarrassed or shy; seek to please God instead of men with what you say. Sure, some will disagree with you but do not be discouraged. Your job is to spread the Word, not accomplish the conversion yourself. Love and be at peace with everyone, including dissenters, and leave the changing of hearts to Jesus.

The work of evangelism is hard, but to shy away from it is to leave room for lies and chaos to fill the spaces where the truth should be. Therefore, boast of the Word and its teachings about Christ. Fear no evil and defend the truth. Embrace your responsibility as one who is saved. Sharing your joy with others and loving others as Jesus loves you is not only a form of thanksgiving and praise but also a way to cause others to wonder what you are so happy about. If you are moved by the power of faith and the constant comfort found in the presence of Christ, you should eagerly tell others about him. The Gospel message is not meant for a few favored ones but for everyone, so share it! May you always be alert and wise about seizing good opportunities to share the Gospel. Amen.

Believe on the Lord Jesus Christ, and you will be saved,
you and your household.

ACTS 16:31

Walk in wisdom toward those who are
outside, redeeming the time.
Let your speech always be with grace, seasoned with salt,
that you may know how you ought to answer each one.

COLOSSIANS 4:5-6

The Lord is not slack concerning His promise,
as some count slackness, but is longsuffering toward us,
not willing that any should perish
but that all should come to repentance.

2 PETER 3:9

Unbelieving Loved Ones

FRIEND, I'M SURE you remember the days when you did not believe. But for the love and concern of a believer who gently introduced you to Christ, you might be lost and doomed to this very day. My heart is filled with joy that you are a believer and we are members of this great community, the Christian church. Let us not forget this is not a secret community but one meant for the world. As believers, we are charged with the role of spreading the Gospel to those who are unbelievers. Jesus instructed us to bring others to him so they may know him.

The blunt truth is not everyone you have ever encountered is in Heaven now or guaranteed to get there. Unbelievers are not there, nor will they ever be. Man without Christ cannot please God because, in unbelief, he cannot do what is pleasing to God. The Scriptures make it clear there are people who are saved and others who are lost. The saved are those who trust Jesus Christ as their eternal Savior. The lost are those who do not trust Christ as Savior. This is most difficult to accept readily, for we both know and love unbelievers. For unbelievers to accept Jesus as Lord and Savior, they must understand the Gospel's primary message. They need to understand how they are born as sinners, and it is only through Christ that they can be saved. And here is the point of this letter – if we genuinely and deeply love them, we will tell them about Jesus.

You must remember that Jesus came to your rescue when you were lost. So now, out of gratitude and love, you are called to find opportunities to do what you can to help others who do not know God, especially among those who are dearest to you. The example Jesus gave you is to build relationships with people who do not know him. When you meet a person who has not yet embraced the truth, you are to have the compassion of Jesus and extend your friendship and grace. Isolating yourself from unbelievers, including strong opposers, misses the point of sharing the good news of Jesus. You were once against God in your unbelief, yet God was gracious to you. Be motivated, then, to share the good news of Christ. And do not just wait for an opportunity to present itself to you; instead, create those opportunities in all you do. Sharing the Gospel is not a hobby or a season but a full-time occupation. For the benefit of those unbelievers you love, this is worthy work to which you must commit yourself.

How do you engage with the unbeliever? Gently and wisely because the reputation of the Gospel depends on you. The world judges Christianity by what it sees in you. Represent it well with kindness, holiness, and reverence to the Lord. Your conduct before an unbeliever should be steeped in grace, your speech overflowing with wisdom. Be humble, loving, caring, kind, and gentle. Your outreach to every person should be fitting to the occasion. Do not hijack a conversation or situation, especially when your audience is not in the mood to listen to you. It is essential to know when not to speak. It is often best to simply listen to someone and wait for a better time. Trust the Holy Spirit; he will guide you in this matter.

I should tell you to prepare yourself for rejection. Christians are called narrow-minded because they believe there is only one way to God, and that is through Jesus Christ. You will be ridiculed, if not outright persecuted, for speaking this truth, perhaps even by members of your own family. Yet, despite these attacks, you are to love and have forbearance. You are not required to convert people; your only requirement is to tell the truth. When you are rejected, insulted, or persecuted, the proper response is to pray for your opposer. In his abundant grace and mercy, God can and will intervene in the lives of unbelievers in response to your prayers. Walk piously among unbelievers so that they may judge you with favor and may themselves be converted to Christ.

Friend, I am not writing only about the unbeliever; I include the lukewarm in my message. Some do not oppose Christ but do not have a passion for him either. Many come from Christian backgrounds and have an idea of who Jesus is but may have never seen the need for him to assure their salvation. They must know that their works and religious practices do not lead to salvation. It is not a thing to be earned. They have to come to know and believe in Jesus. This is where you come in. Remind them that salvation is a gift from God and only by the grace of Jesus Christ.

Before I go, let me remind you that if you truly love anyone, you will tell them about Jesus. Beloved, I urge you to face the people and tell them something worth hearing: how to have an eternal life. People in every corner of the world are looking for a truth that inspires hope. Let them hear it and praise God if anyone is led to Christ. Amen.

Love prospers when a fault is forgiven,
but dwelling on it separates close friends.

PROVERBS 17:9

For if you forgive men their trespasses,
your heavenly Father will also forgive you.
But if you do not forgive men their trespasses,
neither will your Father forgive your trespasses.

MATTHEW 6:14-15

Bear with each other and forgive one another
if any of you has a grievance against someone.
Forgive as the Lord forgave you.

COLOSSIANS 3:13

Forgiveness

MY FRIEND, DO not let the fact that you have been treated wrongly cause you to commit another wrong. Be gentle with those who have wronged you. If you are hard and unforgiving toward others, you are not well-positioned to seek forgiveness for yourself. Having contempt for anyone ultimately only harms you. Remember, you cannot be forgiven if you are one who cannot forgive. Not one of us deserves God's compassion, yet we are forgiven. Christ on the cross prayed for his enemies; remember his example. Just as God forgives you, you should forgive your offenders. When you do, you give glory to God by multiplying his forgiveness. Please do not make it your business to judge and avenge, for as you judge, you too shall be judged. Instead, free yourself from a wrathful mind and strive to live peacefully with everyone. Admit that you, too, have been an offender and ask for forgiveness. Confess your faults as a demonstration of sincere sorrow and accept apologies offered to you with a merciful spirit so that God may be glorified.

Be assured that you are not forgiven only once, but each and every time you repent your sins. So be honest about your imperfections, and you will genuinely find reason to repent each and every day. And remember, mercy begets mercy, and the lack of mercy earns you nothing. Just as you are imperfect, so are those around you. Forgive your neighbors as Jesus forgives you, as often as he forgives you. You are called to be a peace-maker. If you are filled with the love of peace, it must reign in your heart and then rule in your deeds. There must be no disagreement, separation, or rebellion between you and your neighbors, for without peace, no one will see that the love of the Lord dwells in you. Live in peace so that others may see God at work through you. Be gentle to those who have wronged you, and give your family, friends, and neighbors many opportunities to redeem themselves, just as God has forgiven you so many times.

I should point out that forgiving and forgetting are two different things; one is not dependent on the other. Do not confuse forgiving with forgetting. The wrong done to you may be so traumatic that it leaves a scar, an ugly reminder of what has happened. Believe me, the longer you delay forgiving your transgressor, the more painful the scar. But the sooner you genuinely forgive, the quicker the healing and the sooner the trauma becomes a historical fact rather than a present pain. If this seems impossible to you, I urge you to ask a fellow believer to join you in the work that is required to help you wholly and gracefully forgive.

As for you, you may think yourself unworthy of forgiveness. Do not be burdened with shame; you must also be forgiving of yourself. The weight of guilt about your regrettable past is an unholy burden because the ghosts of your transgressions can haunt you into abandoning your renewal. You must let these matters go, or you will not fully enjoy the freedom you have in forgiveness. Your old self, the one from your past and before the time of your renewal, was corrupted by your imperfect judgment and unjust desires. Your new self, guided by righteous obedience, should turn away from all your former sins. Rather than feel shame, rejoice in your redemption! Look ahead, seek the will of God, and have cheer in gratitude for your salvation. Think of yourself with sober judgment but in a spirit of power, love, and self-discipline, one unafraid to be who you have become, one forgiven and saved by grace. Amen!

For we do not have a High Priest
who cannot sympathize with our weaknesses,
but was in all points tempted as we are, yet without sin.
Let us therefore come boldly to the throne of grace,
that we may obtain mercy and find
grace to help in time of need.

HEBREWS 4:15-16

Gratitude

GOD HAS MANY thoughts of love, grace, and mercy concerning you, a sinner such as you are. He has thoughts about your spiritual blessings, your redemption and salvation by Christ, and your eternal life in fellowship with him. God hears your prayers; he listens to your requests and answers them in his own time and according to his judgment of what is best for you. He is a God who bestows favors on you, granting you his presence, indulging you in communion with him, and favoring you with endless supplies of his grace and innumerable mercies. For these and all other things, you should be overflowing with gratitude.

I know that you, a child of God, are grateful, and I pray this characteristic will stay with you all the days of your life. We should always be grateful because the Lord is always with us. Be thankful in all that you do and say, even if you must wait for your heart's desire, for in Christ, you have already received the most precious gift – everlasting life!

Friend, in Christ, you are renewed; by his grace, you were restored. Realize your dependence on him and your complete inability to restore yourself. Do not forget your cleansing. With gratitude, proclaim the work that Christ has performed in and for you. Expressing gratitude honors God and gives him the glory for all that he has done. Gratitude is the realization that all you have and all that you are is a gift from God. Again, you should always be grateful, no matter what your circumstances may be. In practicing constant, conscious gratitude, you will cultivate a heart of thankfulness that will only bring more joy to your life. I want this for you.

My dear friend, give thanks to God in all things with strong affection, sincerity, and a true heart. Be grateful that God is God and that he loves you so much. And please remember that I am so grateful for you and love you so much. Now, please pray for me. That will be a most appreciated reward for the effort I have put into teaching you these things.

And God will wipe away every tear from their eyes;
there shall be no more death, nor sorrow, nor crying.
There shall be no more pain,
for the former things have passed away.

REVELATION 21:4

Heaven

FRIEND, ALL MY letters have been leading up to this, the subject of Heaven. I have led you in this direction along this meandering and occasionally redundant path because I hoped to build excitement in you about what is in store for you as a believer in Christ. And I do not mean only for you, but for me too, because as I said in the beginning, my hope and longing is that we will be together in fellowship in eternity. I care far too much about you to be satisfied having enjoyed your company for only a little while.

So, on to it. What is Heaven? If you imagine Heaven is a place where the streets are paved with gold, the gates are made of pearl, and the walls adorned with precious jewels, you would be right but preoccupied with the wrong things. Focus on this: Heaven is the divine dwelling place of God, an actual realm where everything operates according to his flawless will. Heaven is a place of peace, love, community, and worship, where God is surrounded by a heavenly court and other heavenly beings. It is the very embodiment of God's perfection, where life will be free from death, pain, sickness, disappointment, cruelty, and anything that isn't perfectly lovely. Your future life in Heaven will include the best of the life you now live, plus additional joys far beyond your imagination.

The Lord Jesus is in Heaven, at the right hand of the Father, making intersession for you and me just now as you read this letter. Myriads of angels are in Heaven, too, serving the Lord in various ways. And the saints of God who died on Earth are in Heaven. Everyone who has genuinely trusted in Christ as Lord and Savior will be there, including those we dearly love and who have given themselves to Jesus. What wonderful company we shall have! And in Heaven, God will know us as we truly are, inside and out, past and present, with nothing hidden but everything known. When we awake in Heaven, we will know each other as God knows us because all the secrets and flaws of this life will have been removed. In this life, sin has caused us to deceive others and ourselves in a vain effort to hide our misdeeds. But when we are finally freed from the influence of sin, then we can be as we were created to be, without sin, shame, and embarrassment. No one will begrudge us for any reason because everyone will love each other in the same unconditional loving way that Jesus loves you today. I am so eager to present myself to you in this cleansed and redeemed state, for as good a friend as I have tried to be, I know I have offended or disappointed you from time to time.

Best of all, let's not overlook this: in Heaven, we will see Jesus himself face to face. We will worship the Son of God and praise his great victory over sin and death in his very presence! The best worship you have experienced on Earth will pale in comparison to the celebration you will enjoy at the feet of your Savior. How wonderful it will be to walk with him literally!

Do I know all there is to know about Heaven? No, but I am sure of this one truth. No one will go to Heaven except by the grace of God and through the merits of the sacrifice of Jesus Christ. Without Jesus, you have no hope of seeing Heaven. Friend, if you know Jesus, you have nothing to fear. So put your trust in Jesus. Stand with your full weight on the merit of the author and finisher of your salvation. May God help you to trust in Jesus Christ and him alone for your salvation. May God grant that we will meet again in Heaven one day. Amen!

P.S.

MY BELOVED FRIEND, do not think I am so clever that I was able to write these letters to you exclusively from my heart and imagination. I wish it were true, but it is not. Most of what I have written to you is wisdom and understanding developed during years of Bible study, worship and fellowship with other believers, and time spent in prayer. Yes, I have had revelations about the truth, but not one came out of thin air. All were the reward for spending time in pursuit of a more righteous relationship with God. Please do not let your pursuit of a righteous relationship with God be limited to the reading and contemplation of my letters to you. Instead, spend time reading the Bible, for "All Scripture is given by inspiration of God, and is profitable for doctrine, for reproof, for correction, for instruction in righteousness, that the man of God may be complete, thoroughly equipped for every good work," (2 Timothy 3:16-17).

Read it many times, for once is certainly not enough to grasp the whole of it. Spend time with believers who are more mature in the faith than you are. Spend time on your knees in fervent prayer. Do these things, and you will learn and understand so much more than what I can teach you in a few thousand words.

Most of all, remember this — the Christian life is not as complicated as it may seem. It requires only two things of you: to love God with all your heart, soul, strength, and mind, and to love your neighbor as yourself. Let these be your nature and daily habit; everything else will take care of itself in due time. Until we are together again, may the Prince of Peace be with you always. Amen!

Now may the God of peace who brought up our Lord Jesus from the dead, the great shepherd of the sheep, by the blood of the eternal covenant, equip you with everything good that you may do his will, working in you that which is pleasing in his sight, through Jesus Christ,

to whom be glory forever and ever. Amen.

HEBREWS 13:20-21

To contact the author: gregoryelang@gmail.com

In composing these letters, the author was inspired by writings from these sources in the public domain:

Commentary Critical and Explanatory on the Whole Bible

Geneva Study Bible

John Darby's Synopsis of the New Testament

John Gill's Exposition of the Bible

Matthew Henry Commentary on the Whole Bible

People's New Testament

About the Author

Resembling a collection of letters written to friends and loved ones, Gregory E. Lang breaks down complex scriptural messages to share insight and encouragement with his readers. He prompts them to live more intentional lives that honor God and build harmony with their fellow citizens.

As a leader in the charitable healthcare sector in Georgia, Greg served as the executive officer of a Christian nonprofit organization serving the poor of the metropolitan Atlanta area. He has spent more than a decade teaching those mature and young in the Christian faith the practical application in daily living and the workplace of Biblical lessons about how God's creation was meant to live and relate to one another. A New York Times bestselling author, Greg published his first book in 2002 and continues to write advice, inspiration, and Christian devotion literature. His cumulative sales record is 6.5 million copies, and he has appeared on the New York Times Best Seller list seventeen times.